GENIUS IN 21 DAYS

Learn faster with secrets to unlimited productivity

COSIMO INTERMITE

To Jonathan

To your small pe-s

Keep your genius inside.

You're a genius without knowing geography

Love your energy!

Genius in 21 Days
Learn faster with secrets to unlimited productivity
By Cosimo Intermite

Companion website at www.geniusin21daysusa.com

Editor: Pagetrim Book Services

ISBN: 978-1-64810-215-8

Published by Perfect Publishing, Co.

"Nothing happens unless first you dream"
Carl Sandburg

"Believe in your dreams and they will believe in you"
Cosimo Intermite

About the Author

His teacher once said, "Cosimo, being dyslexic and having learning disabilities, you can't go that far, you have to adapt!"

Now a world-renowned expert in advanced learning techniques, memory improvement, brain optimization, and accelerated learning, Cosimo has proved that learning difficulties are no constraint to becoming successful and that his teacher needs to improve his motivational skills. He has used his expertise as a brain coach to students, seniors, entrepreneurs, and educators for over twelve years.

Born and bred in the south of Italy, he moved to the US with his wife and never looked back. In fact, within four weeks of migrating, he held his first course on the techniques he used to learn English in just two weeks, drawing on his studies concerning learning styles and techniques that consisted of 6,000 words and grammar rules.

He is considered a learning expert in his field with master-level qualifications in Mind Maps, Speed Reading, Micro-Facial Expressions, Team-building, Public Speaking, Effective Communication, Goal Setting, Decision-making, Personal Development, Time Management, and Memory Techniques.

Co-Creator of the Genius in 21 Days course, available in 50+ countries with over 520 face-to-face and 600 virtual classes delivered every year, his impact on the student community has reached epic proportions.

In his free time, he enjoys the simple things in life; reading, meditating, traveling, spending quality time with family and playing hide-and-seek with his wonderful two-year-old daughter, providing both stimulation and relaxation to the mind – the most powerful tool in the world.

Cosimo's partner, Stephanie, is the co-creator of Genius in 21 Days. As a mom, wife and successful business creator, when they told Stephanie, "Women are supposed to stay at home and men are supposed to work!" she replied, "Are you still living in caves?"

Now a world-renowned expert in advanced learning techniques, memory improvement, brain optimization, and accelerated learning as well as a mom, wife and successful businesswoman who started everything and made Genius In 21 Days in the US possible, you could argue that Stephanie is a modern-day Wonder Woman. When she came to the US alone with her bags and her ingenuity, she had "a dream and a big heart." That's what she says, and she managed the students all by herself.

She started working with Genius In 21 Days in Italy in 2013 in the customer service department, but her leadership and dedication earned her a partnership with the company a few years later.

Like her husband, Cosimo, she is a learning expert in this field with master-level qualifications in Mind Maps, Speed Reading, Micro-Facial Expressions, Team- building, Public Speaking, Effective Communication, Goal Setting, Decision-making, Personal Development, Time Management, and Memory Techniques.

As an author and public speaker, she empowers all women around the world and helps them find their inspiration. "When you feel things are falling on you and you are the only one who can catch them, when things are not going as planned and the only thing you see is a huge obstacle that you don't know how to overcome, these are the moments in which you need to have faith, know everything is perfect, and one day you'll know exactly why things were happening for you. Show yourself how strong you are and find your way. You are greatness, sometimes we just need something or someone to remind us."

Stephanie was born and grew up in Cantù, a small town in northern Italy. She attended college in Lugano, Switzerland, and majored in business communication. During the last year of school, she attended the Genius in 21 Days course and learned some amazing techniques that allowed her to be more efficient and save time while studying.

In her free time, she enjoys the simple things in life; reading, cooking, traveling, sports (especially basketball), spending quality time with friends and family and playing hide-and-seek with her husband and wonderful daughter.

Foreword – Bob Snyder

Over the last thirty-five years, I have built dozens of companies that have produced hundreds of millions in sales. Through these companies we have trained tens of thousands of individuals in business, finance, and real estate investing. The key to each student's success has been their ability to learn, retain and apply the lessons taught. My own investing career started decades ago, and I will never forget the advice from one of my first rea estate mentors, who often impressed upon me that the most valuable real estate I would ever invest in was the six inches between my ears. It's a fact that whether you're climbing the corporate ladder, building a business empire, or striving towards getting a college degree, an investment in yourself pays the highest rate of return. It's also an asset that can't be taken from you in a bad economy or failed business transaction.

It's a valuable resource that can help you to repeat success over and over again and can help you to acquire the competency and confidence to overcome life's obstacles. I'm also a big believer in the fact education is the key to eradicating poverty, assisting with the demands of raising children, empowering us to elect competent and honest government officials, minimizing the risk of investing and increasing the probability of success in the business world. Genius in 21 Days by Cosimo and Stephanie taught us to learn, retain and apply all education, increasing our ability tenfold. It's been a game-changer for our students, and I am confident it will be for anyone immersing themselves in this revolutionary system.

I believe everyone should read this book. It contains the processes, understanding, and plans to help people from all walks of life improve their learning, retention, comprehension, and reading skills.

I am so impressed by the Genius in 21 Days system that I have promoted it to all our students. I mentioned earlier that this system is a game-changer for the individual but also companies, religious organizations, schools, and government's. The list goes on and on because anyone who wants to learn anything can benefit from these time-tested processes. When businesses, organizations, and groups encourage their people to understand these processes and techniques, it improves efficiencies and, in many cases, profits for the organization as a whole.

I know I've said some flattering things about my experience. I'm what you call a raving fan, but don't take my word for it. Read this book and see for yourself what Genius in 21 Days can do for you. It might just be the best thing you've ever done for yourself or your company.

Bob Snyder
Renatus Founder and CEO

Contents

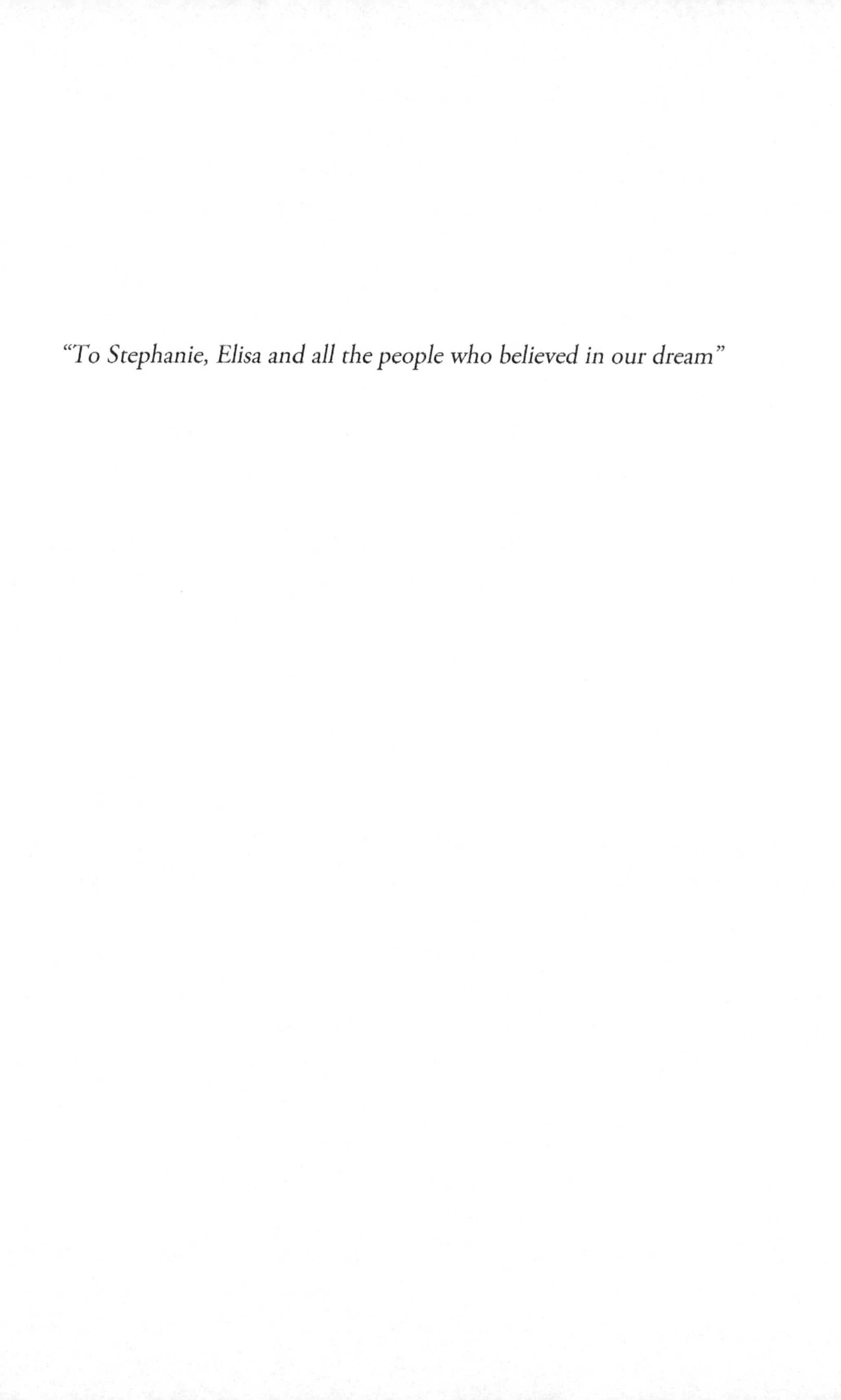

"To Stephanie, Elisa and all the people who believed in our dream"

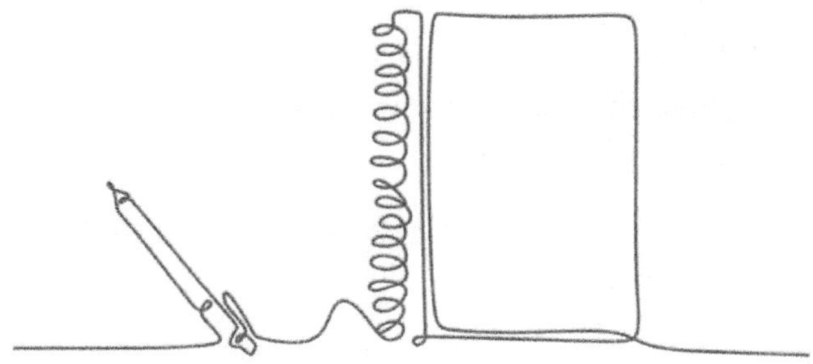

Chapter 1
Introduction

I am glad you are in front of these pages. Hopefully, you will be reading this with big expectations since it will be the beginning of positive **new results in your studies and work.**

I will explain how to create your own study method and an effective work method during each phase so you can dramatically improve your results. All you have to do is follow my instructions step by step and at the end of this process, you will have your perfect method, allowing you to achieve whatever you want. The sky's the limit!

Excellence is a habit, not a result. To achieve success and excellence when you study or work, you have to adopt the tools that will lead you to your goal.

Why This Book?

If you are a professional

No one told us how to learn, only what to learn, and that's why you developed different blocks in learning. When we feel overwhelmed, frustrated, anxious, fearful and doubtful of performance and outcomes in business, it's not because you are not good enough or have fewer skills than others. It's not really you but a learning block you acquired in school that' still affects you in your business life. Maybe so much time has passed since school, and you can't relate or link the learning block from school, but think about this:

Did the teachers ever tell you how your brain likes organizing projects, clients, follow-ups, and your life? You left school by studying last minute and doing your best to be ready. This is the learning block of procrastination.

Did they ever tell you how your brain likes understanding new concepts you can find to expand your business? You needed to read over and over before you could retain anything – they only gave you repetition and warnings to pay attention.

Did they ever tell you how your brain likes being focused?

Did they ever tell you how your brain likes working for you in business?

My answer to all these questions was NO! I mean, I can find a way to organize myself, but why am I feeling this overwhelmed or limited to new things I really want to do? If you don't know how your brain works, how can you create and work effectively with it?

LACK OF METHOD = LACK OF CONFIDENCE

A method is a series of tools, techniques, and strategies that, once applied, you achieve a certain result. It's knowing "HOW TO create a result." So, having a method eliminates the feeling of being overwhelmed, anxious, frustrated or riddled with fear because having a method creates confidence.

You shouldn't feel overwhelmed if you have a method.

You shouldn't feel frustrated if you have a method and know-how.

But when you have a method, you should feel confident. Let's build a perfect method once and forever. I don't think that when you finish school, you finish learning. We are all lifelong learners. You never stop learning, and those who think you do are blinkered to reality and likely to achieve little moving forward. As a businessman, I needed to keep learning every day, but faster than when I was at school. I don't know about you, but I never stopped learning.

For this reason, whenever you come across the word class or school during this book, tweak it based on your profession. For example, if you are never in class or school, think of the words conference and meeting, whenever you see the words professor or teacher, if you never have a professor or teacher, think of the word boss, colleague or mentor. Also, when you find the word exam and you never need to take an exam, think of it as a goal you have, a project, something you want to learn for yourself. Remember, we're all students all the time.

You will find a lost version of yourself in school, a young child who was never taught HOW your brain likes learning. In my opinion, it's a wasted opportunity and a tragic shame.

If you are a student

Switching from high school to college or university can be like entering a new world where everything is new and unfamiliar. The high school teacher who was always there to tell you what to study is no longer part of your support network. You were forced to attend classes and meet institutional expectations to make an effort to obtain good grades.

Now you have entered the world of studying all day and night.

When you become a college student or take courses or a master's degree, you are no longer forced to attend classes. The responsibility, therefore, lies with you to manage your study habits and attendance. You go from a small teacher-led class to a large anonymous class, listening to a teacher who probably doesn't even know your name.

In addition, the difficulty level of study increases tenfold. The more relaxed environment and onus on you to be diligent and focused is more difficult. Your attention span is shorter, and other commitments in your life may distract you: relationships, part-time jobs, and team sports. Then, at the end of class, you find yourself with infinite work, notes and books full of technical concepts that you have to learn and memorize.

In high school, you can build bonds with the teachers and know what to expect during and outside of class, helping you to prepare for important exams. At college, teacher-student relationships are more impersonal, and the exams are often high-stakes as if they were finals, meaning you cannot go into them ill-prepared.

This instability, subject to the unpredictability, generates major problems in American universities with a dropout rate of 32.9%. First-year students have a twelve-month dropout rate of 24.1%. 58% of American students take over six or more years to complete college. Those who do manage to graduate are often one year late in best-case scenarios. As a result, frequent career changes are not uncommon.

Metaphorically speaking, this problem originates from having studied in a fishbowl for twelve years, and then jumping into the ocean without a life jacket.

Of course, this affects your results!

Conclusion

This is why we have dedicated the last twenty years to helping entrepreneurs, CEOs, companies, students and anyone who loves learning but doesn't have a method to improve their working skills and study behaviors and achieve better results in their business or during their academic years.

This book contains two decades' worth of knowledge and experience, and I am delighted to share this with you.

This is why we have dedicated the last twenty years to helping entrepreneurs, CEOs and companies to create a perfect method to never feel overwhelmed or stressed. To improve their productive skills, organizational and focusing abilities and how to become "un-distractable" by switching their brain state to the task at hand and "getting in the zone." The aim is to be at least 50% more productive right after the course.

Students improve their study behaviors and achieve better academic results.

Imagine you buy a wardrobe at IKEA, take it home, unbox it and find a number of parts, screws, and keys for perfectly assembling a spaceship. Great, but it means nothing without step-by-step instructions. That is why IKEA furniture always includes a manual. Now, hypothetically, imagine you don't have the manual: all those planks of wood and screws are of no use to you. But what if you bought the wrong manual? You would try to assemble an entirely different piece of furniture with the pieces of a wardrobe. Put another way, you would be wasting your time and energy.

EITHER

You have entered the entrepreneurial world with the wrong manual. You are doing your best with the resources you have, but to-do lists, calendars or other apps are not working to manage everything you want to create. You may want to be a great public speaker, but you don't retain or organize your ideas well.

OR

You have just entered college or university with the wrong manual. You have the high school study manual, trying to study 300 pages with only 20 that are actually effective.

That is why we have created Genius in 21 Days. It will teach you everything you need to be a self-sufficient entrepreneur who feels confident and relaxed knowing they will achieve their results without stress, enjoy family vacations without a nagging conscience of things to do, own their time and not be slaves to their business. And self-sufficient students get top results, graduate quickly, and enjoy a balanced social/study life without experiencing helplessness, frustration or criticism. To achieve this, I will teach you how to overcome specific obstacles that include:

- ✓ concentration
- ✓ procrastination
- ✓ dips in motivation
- ✓ overcoming boredom
- ✓ eliminating exam stress
- ✓ public speaking stress

Who am I to Tell You How to Study?

I have dedicated my life to better understanding advanced learning for over twelve years. But I started out like you, as a student of engineering. At that time, I wanted to be an electrical engineer. I wanted to finish my degree quickly so I could dedicate myself to my chosen industry and start building my life. However, when I started my degree and realized how much I had to study for the next four years, I became a little overwhelmed and started doubting my ability to learn it all. Luckily, my attitude changed when I signed up for a memory and speed-reading course called Magister. That's where I met Luca Lorenzoni, who taught me how to transform my results when studying.

I realized that studying could be much easier than I thought. And it was. I began passing my exams with excellent grades by studying techniques that would have taken months in just three weeks. When my colleagues and friends witnessed this change, they became curious and wanted to know the secret. That's when I realized how much I wanted to help people achieve the same quality results. It wasn't as easy as I thought, though. Not everything works for everyone as people learn differently. Individuals must adapt their study methods to suit their own personalities and learning styles. There is no one-size-fits-all approach.

After twelve years, I have fulfilled my dream: to help thousands of people achieve positive results through a customized method that meets every individual's needs.

Therefore, when someone asks me what I like most about what I do, my answer is always the same: to help people achieve results beyond their expectations. I strive to help them reach the turning point where they realize they have achieved the impossible, such as learning to speak a language in just one month or passing exams with top grades and no stress.

This sparks new dreams because you begin to ask yourself "What other crazy accomplishments can I add to my resume?"

Instruction Manual

Throughout this manual, I will guide you step by step, just like the assembly of your IKEA wardrobe, but with the correct manual using the ideal method for you. I will explain how to customize it based on your personality and current studies.

I advise you to read this manual first for a holistic overview (I will delve into this later), without spending too much time taking notes and trying out the techniques so that you can get an idea of the method. Then start over and do a second reading, this time analytically, focusing on the details and, above all, being selective about what you learn, as if it were a book you had to study at college.

If, after reading this the first time, you feel you do not need to see the overview because what you are eager to get cracking with the techniques, I advise you to at least look at the index so you can see how many chapters and pages there are and what you will find inside each one. Only then should you start reading and advance sequentially, preferably putting into practice the techniques you find in each phase.

Whether you prefer to read it holistically (first) or analytically (second), you can apply the techniques depending on your situation and needs. For example, if you want to increase your reading speed, you can go directly to that chapter and start putting the techniques and exercises into practice. Everything I will teach you can be tested directly on your current studies.

So, are you ready to create your own personal instruction manual tailored to your work and studies so you know what to do in each phase? Okay, then let's begin!

The Education Trap System

As soon as your studies begin, you find yourself in no-man's-land, awkwardly traversing the academic landscape and trying to find your feet in this new, unfamiliar territory. Unless you were fortunate enough to have a friend in the same higher education course who could provide you with insight into what your course entails, you're in for a bumpy ride with a few bitter surprises thrown in.

Classes are longer with some teachers reading a series of mind-numbing slides, leaving you with heavy eyelids and fifty new pages to study. Repeat this for each subject every day, fifty pages a day for three or four months, and you will be begging for the sweet release of death. That's because no one has taught you how to effectively learn and obtain all that information.

Here are three effective study secrets that form the basis for you to successfully progress in your degree:

Secret 1. The method you used during school no longer works. At most, you had twenty pages to study for a test. Spending a day reading and memorizing the information was relatively easy, and you didn't have to dig deep or try too hard to pass the exam. When selectivity arrives, they ask you to remember what you studied last September, a challenge for anyone. At selectivity or university, you now have 200 pages to process and store. This, to put it bluntly, is not realistic. You get stressed processing so many details and technical concepts that you must memorize. That's why this high school method doesn't work now, and you need a better and more suitable blueprint. Plus, how many details do we have to process and organize when working on a project, for example? Since high school, our methods have been the same. But now we are achieving goals in our business that are different from high school goals. How can we achieve business goals by using high school ways of organizing, studying or thinking? That's why we feel stressed.

Secret 2. You need a study method. You need a method that allows you to effectively learn and retain a large amount of information in a short time, regardless of the degree or business goal you are pursuing. The information is relentless, changing every few months, depending on technology upgrades, market demands, or your study schedule if you're a student. Every time a new subject begins, it is like starting from scratch. For that reason, when I talk about learning, I mean understanding and knowing how to use the information you study.

Secret 3. Each person is different. You need a method that suits you. It must be adapted to your traits, attention span, needs and obligations. It has to adapt to your way of learning, how you communicate and your cognitive style (more on this during the following chapters). This way, you can utilize them and adopt a study method tailored to you.

Now that you know these study secrets, let's find out what the next steps are. Buckle up, this is going to be fun!

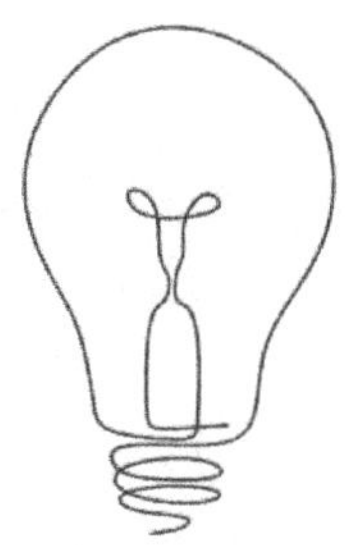

Chapter 2
The Next Steps

The 2 to 6 Phase Leap: ARCORE

How to relegate the 2-phase method of Read and Repeat used in high school and adopt ARCORE.

Each letter of ARCORE stands for every step of the study method that will completely change your way of studying. So, what does ARCORE stand for?

A: APPROACH.

Have you heard the saying, "well begun is half done?" Well, the approach refers to the way you study.

To begin well means with a proper state of mind by analyzing your feelings towards that subject.

The temple: in this phase, we also discuss how to create the ideal environment to study and focus.

The master plan: how to manage your time effectively and avoid procrastination or being overwhelmed. One of the most common mistakes when revising for an exam is to divide the pages or chapters by days since not all contain the same level of difficulty. In fact, topics generally become harder as you progress, so you have to distribute your time proportionally.

Study cycles: how long to study, when to take a break, and when to re-read.

How to set goals that are exciting and easy to achieve.

R: READING

- Focusing techniques. If you don't manage to focus, you will end up wasting a lot of time and succumbing to the distractions around you.

No distractions: how to avoid distractions down to the finest detail.

Strategic reading: how to read faster while absorbing and understanding everything.

C: COMPREHENSION

Sometimes, you may believe you zone out, and that's why you do not understand what you read, but it is the other way around. When you do not understand something is when you get distracted and lose momentum. That is why it is essential to master this step.

How to understand even the most complex books on the first attempt.

Re-learn how to highlight.

Learn the language of your resources and professors.

O: ORGANIZATION

Keywords are the new summary.

There's a different strategy for each subject.

Take notes and create schemes without having to re-write what you read.

R: RETENTION

Memory techniques that suit your cognitive style.

Mnemonic devices for you to learn faster.

- Remember long term.

E: EXPOSURE - How to effectively Present

How to deal with stress.

Public speaking techniques.

Body language techniques.

There is No One Exactly Like You

I've never seen two students who learn the same way. Indeed, we all have our quirks and habits, but I'm sure you will identify yourself in one of the following six categories. For each category, there is a specific technique for using this manual and immediately taking advantage of it. So, to which category do you belong?

1. The student who dedicates their time to get good results but has to sacrifice something they like:

Imagine you are a student doing very well, enjoying your studies but have to spend too many hours to earn good grades. As a result, you have to give up sports and cannot socialize with friends and family often. If you are working, you can now understand that you created a learning block that makes you think I have to spend hours and work hard to get results, sacrificing personal and family time.

The goal, therefore, is to find a method that sees you getting the same quality results but way faster so you have more free time to do the things you enjoy. If you can relate to this category, it means you are capable of understanding the information and processing it, you simply need to optimize the process so you can strike a balance between your social life and study commitments. Stay tuned for the chapters on what to do to study faster and work effectively.

2. The student who relies on motivation:

Your **extrinsic motivation** to get that degree, start working in your desired career, escape your family always asking you how your studies and work are going, or avoid wasting time or repeating subjects that drive you to study hard. This is the kind of student who dedicates their time to study but does not get their desired results. It could be that you freeze or go blank during an exam, even though you studied hard because you are nervous. Maybe you spend too many hours with your head in your books but constantly lose focus, causing you to waste precious time. Maybe you have a hard time memorizing data and forget quickly. And despite all your effort, energy and time, there is always something that prevents you from getting the grades you want. In the **professional** world, this translates to feeling frustrated no matter how much or how hard you try, we keep losing focus, becoming forgetful. And despite all your effort, energy and time, there is always something that prevents you from getting the results you want.

If you see yourself in this category, it is because you try hard and give everything but still fall short of the results you seek. This is a personal quality that we will take advantage of during this book. With my advice for you, it will be easy to study and improve. What if your problem is stress and a lack of focus? If so, by applying the recommended techniques designed for this type of learner and applying it to your studies and work, you should start to see dramatic results in your ability to maintain focus, improve time management, and overcome any debilitating nervousness during examinations.

3. The student who wants to graduate and achieve career goals but does not feel like studying or working, thinking they're lazy:

The truth is you're not lazy at all. Do you enjoy going to the movies or a good Friday night out? Maybe you like to party or have a drink. These are all signs that you do not fall into the 'lazy' category!

Of course, nobody wants to do something they are not good at. Why continue bachata classes if you fall every time you dance? The same logic applies to studying. If you don't see results after trying very hard, you grow tired and lose motivation. Imagine if studying became easy and fast. I bet your attitude would change.

I advise you to read the entire book, focusing on the chapter where I explain how to have the desire to study or work. If you are not enthusiastic about applying a new method that will help you work or study faster and easier and do not focus on trying to figure out how to have more desire to study or work, it will be impossible to boost your results. It does not matter if you have been led to believe you are lazy; the past does not reflect the future.

4. The student who achieves good results with no sacrifices. These are very ambitious people but don't know what they could do better:

To dismiss all modesty here, you have found the perfect book. Before you start reading, I advise you to ask yourself what extraordinary results you would like to achieve. Imagine you are doing great in college or your career and have the time to go out, do sports, or go on vacation with your family for as long as you want. Being a person with so many skills, you could consider learning two more languages this year, do more certifications or graduating six months earlier, or perhaps creating your CV in a way that gets you any job you want. If you can relate to this, I advise you to take a pen and paper and start dreaming. Ask yourself what you would do if you had superpowers.

5. The student doing well but would like to get better grades:

Are you someone who gets by with good grades and no more or who gets good grades but could score higher? At work, are you someone who gets by with good results and no more or someone who gets good results but could achieve more? If you exist in this 4th category, where average and mediocrity sum up your overall performance, the focus is not how to use this manual to learn two more languages this year but how you can continue doing everything you do today and obtain better results in work and school.

6. Those who can't make up their mind:

You feel you have chosen the wrong career, either because you are fulfilling your parents' wishes, or because it is the option with "more job prospects" even though it is not what you are passionate about.

For example, if you have chosen law because you wanted to please your parents, I advise you to use this book before changing your mind. Give yourself one more semester to try and pass all the exams with high marks without having to sacrifice anything. Once you reach a point where you can do law easily, sit down and re-evaluate your situation. You might find your newfound skills and expertise have become your purpose in life.

If you're working for a company because the pay is high and the job is secure but you want to have your own business, give yourself the possibility to build another "side gig" that generates money until it can substitute your job. Use your current job to feed your dream job and your focus, emotions, and reasons for going to work will change.

Instead of running away from your difficulties, turn and face them or it will become an unshakeable habit in life. You have to challenge yourself and learn to take responsibility to be successful in life. Of course, if you still want to change your path, go ahead with a clear conscience.

Understanding what type of student you are allows you to become aware of how we have blocks in learning affecting us when we are working and, with the aid of this instruction manual, tackle what is really important to you.

Tell Me What Your Method is and I'll Tell You What Your Results are

If you judge a fish by its ability to climb trees, it will think that it is useless for the rest of its life. Albert Einstein.

We are different, it is a fact. We have different mindsets, different attributes, and different ambitions. It's the same with our way of learning. We have different cognitive styles (learning styles) and communicative channels through which we assimilate different information. And this changes everything.

If you have been in a class with a teacher who you did not understand, with whom you had conflicting opinions, that subject was probably no good for you. On the contrary, the same occurs if you have a teacher with whom everything clicked and you got along famously, it is not necessarily due to their teaching skills.

The answer has always been staring you in the face, but until now "understanding" a subject or teacher was a matter of luck.

The truth is it has always depended on how you communicate and receive information. It relates to compatibility.

It's like trying to speak Spanish with a Thai person. The languages are not compatible.

Your teachers, trainers, supervisors and managers, like you, are used to transmitting and receiving information in their own way, according to their styles. The problem is that sometimes incompatibility occurs because you are doing it through different channels. That's why some subjects and classes are unintelligible to you, because they are incompatible, while your classmate has understood everything perfectly.

You can't always keep everyone happy.

This does not mean you have to throw in the towel. I am not giving you the licence to give up on classes and your teachers. What I am going to teach you will help you understand them and understand better, to catch their tricks, and take control of what you study and work on.

They are called communication channels and cognitive styles, and no matter how technical they sound, everyone uses them all the time, even when we publish content on our social networks.

What is a communication channel? It is like a filter through which all the information we receive passes. Imagine a door through which only red cars of a single make can enter and exit.

These doors, or channels, through which we receive and encode information, consist mainly of two: the visual channel and the verbal channel. I will describe them so you can identify yours!

Visual:

When you study or do something information-related, even just to travel, you have a preference for colors, drawings, images, shapes, arrows, symbols, and graphics. You prefer books full of images than full of text.

Verbal:

If you fall under verbal, you have a preference for texts, written explanations, listening in class, taking notes and detailed explanations. You prefer the images and graphics to come with a caption or clarification.

Are you more visual or verbal? It is also possible that you have a little of both. It is normal as we all have both channels, but as a general rule, we use one more than the other when we study. So, identify yours because it will be fundamental for creating your ideal study method during the book.

But it does not end here because, in addition to an input and output channel, we also have our own style of processing that information. This is called cognitive style.

What is a Cognitive Style?

It's the way your brain makes information. Taking the previous red car analogy, it is how you use that car, whether you are slower or faster, and your ability to put its functions into practice. Let's see them!

Analytical:

When you study, talk or perform some other activity, you usually look for all the possible details, get to the core of the issue even if that means drowning in books and notes. If you have to explain something, you count on the commas, and it is difficult to settle on what you know for an exam because you may have missed an exclamation mark.

Global:

If you are global, you need to know the gist of the study. Before going into detail and looking for the cat's five legs, you need to have a general idea of what the class or chapter you will study will be about, otherwise you get lost. It's like when you go to the cinema, you need to see the trailer before the movie.

Not in vain, we have called a technique that you will find in chapter 4 "the trailer technique," especially for global learners.

So, are you analytical or global?

How about your teachers, peers or even your parents, are they analytical or global, verbal or visual? Something to think about!

Now that you know how to identify them, pay attention to how they speak and how they explain things. Imagine you are global and have an analytical teacher or manager who explains everything in the finest detail without describing the points they will deal with. To combat this, you will have to look at the text before class so you do not get lost during the lecture.

It will also help you when you have to talk to them; if you know that they are global and you are analytical, first create a plan in your mind before going into the crux of what you want to say, explain the exact reason for your conversation so it will be easier for them to understand.

The more you familiarize yourself with this, the easier it will be to take advantage of your classes, subjects and relationships with friends and family because, suddenly, you will start speaking a compatible language.

Throughout this book, for each study phase, I will teach you what techniques to apply according to your cognitive styles. Are you ready to delve into the first phase? Great, let's go!

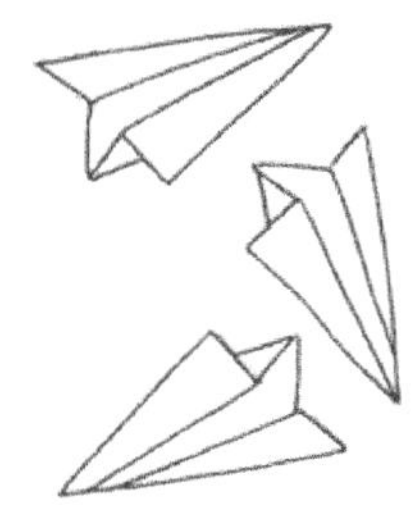

Chapter 3
A For Approach

The first phase of the ARCORE method corresponds to the letter A, which refers to the approximation. In this chapter, we will discuss everything related to study or work preparation, for example, where to study, ideal environments and their characteristics, and how to create the optimal study space. But just knowing this is not enough. You need to know the ideal study duration, when and how to study, how to make breaks and where to do reviews. You will also learn how to create achievable goals that will lead you to obtain the desired results. I will teach you how to create a master plan to organize yourself and not leave everything to the last minute. For example, if you have a 500-page exam, would you know how to divide them, how to choose what to study today and what to leave for another day? Or identify the central themes? Or if you have an important project to finish, how do you really schedule your time?

Your attitude towards this book will determine the quality of the results you will achieve, so the first step is to debunk the myth that "I am not good at studying."

I'm No Good At It

When it comes to learning a subject, what sometimes begins as a small challenge can snowball into a more serious problem. For example, if we make mistake after mistake, we convince ourselves that a certain discipline is not for us. We continue to make mistakes and do not understand that mistakes are part of the normal learning process.

We begin to associate this matter with pain and fear of failure and criticism. A diabolical mechanism is activated in the mind in the face of a pending task, whereby we have to face two difficulties: the difficulty with the test and the fear of making mistakes, naturally predisposing us to failure.

It happens in all areas. **How many times have you struggled to understand a subject fundamental to your career?**

This is how "acquired disability" is born. We convince ourselves that we do not know how to do something. We associate this inability with our way of being, our identity, and perceive it as part of ourselves, something personal and persistent that invades us. It becomes the default setting: "I am not good at it" and we resign.

The fault lies with the three P's, because we believe that our inability is:

Personal, that is, associated with our identity. We conceive of our incapacity as something written in our DNA.

Permanent, because we feel that it is impossible to change this situation and, therefore, believe that we cannot improve.

Penetrating, because the general conviction that we are not good enough can invade all areas of our lives.

The acquired incapacity originates in the "limiting beliefs" – thoughts that diminish personal power and convince us we have less potential than we actually possess.

We all activate strategies that allow us to avoid disappointment in the face of possible failure, but in doing so, we run the risk of being blocked because we make the mistake of associating our personal value with the quality of the results obtained.

Is it enough to believe in it with all your strength?

Limiting beliefs undermine security and prevent us from expressing all our capabilities. However, the negative mental mechanism that causes the most difficulties can become positive and generate "empowering beliefs" that allow us to make the most of our abilities.

This mechanism is based on the following formula:

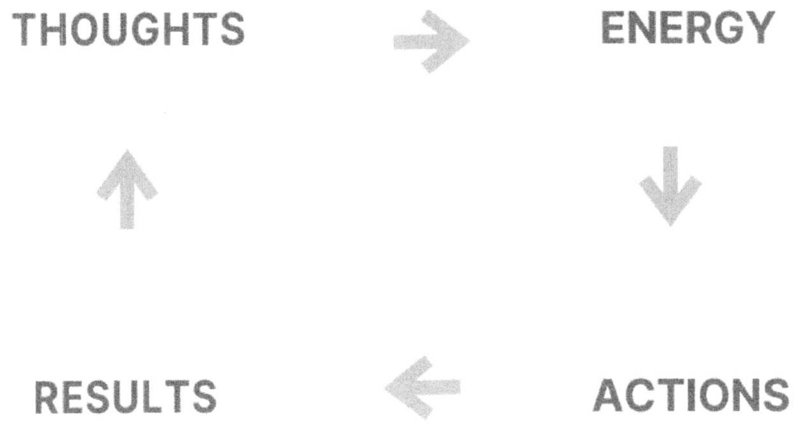

The formula reads as follows: "A person's results are the fruits of his actions, influenced by their energy and emotional state, directly linked to the type of thoughts they have about themselves in what they are doing." Or, to put it simply: your thoughts create your results.

What You Believe, You Create

The set of beliefs that constitute the learning model of each person is formed, in the first place, by the information and programming received in the past, especially in the first years of life.

The main sources are perhaps obvious: parents, siblings, friends, teachers or authorities in various fields such as media, culture, and religion. Every child is taught how to think and act, and these teachings constitute their conditioning and programming. Thus, each child acquires a belief system, which translates into automatic responses valid for life, or at least until someone decides to intervene by actively participating and changing their beliefs.

Experiences of the past that condition the present:

Thoughts generate different emotions, and influences the quality and quantity of actions we undertake to obtain a certain type of result.

So where do these thoughts come from? And why do different people attribute completely different meanings to the same fact?

Thoughts are born from experiences, programming, and conditioning received in the past. Thus, to obtain results, we must change our conditioning or programming if they are ineffective or unproductive.

Conditioning usually occurs in three ways:

1. **Verbal programming:** what you were told about a certain topic when you were little. For example, how did they talk about your general aptitude for study, reading, and culture? All the affirmations you received remain in your subconscious and contribute to forming your beliefs about the subject.
2. **Modeling:** what you've seen and done. Children learn almost everything through imitation and emulation. Think about what your parents' or guardians' attitude to learning was.

3. Specific episodes: what you have personally experienced. We have all experienced concrete events that have consolidated the fundamental beliefs of our way of thinking. What were the most significant experiences in the field of learning? What relationships did you have with your teachers and peers? What emotions were linked to the study?

Since experiences forge convictions and beliefs, it is important to look for those past events that are conditioning the choices and sensations of the present because the only important thing about a fact is the meaning we attribute to it. Becoming aware of this is necessary to enact change.

Change Perspective

How to change a negative attitude? Four key elements can set change in motion. Each one is essential to reprogramming the way we learn.

The first is consciousness: it is impossible to change something without first knowing its existence. We must identify the personal obstacles (i.e., beliefs) that prevent us from achieving our goals; only then can we bring them down.

The second is understanding: if we can understand where our way of thinking comes from, we will realize that it is external factors. Therefore, it is not an intrinsic characteristic and as such is insurmountable.

The third is dissociation: when we understand that this way of thinking disadvantages us and causes us pain, the mind perceives the need to distance itself, but only if we want to obtain better results. It is easier to do this if we begin to observe our way of thinking for what it really is - a "programming document" stored in our mind a long time ago, which may no longer have any value or truth.

The fourth and final element of change is reconditioning. Those who attend my learning courses realize what they can achieve by applying the method. Reaping the emotional rewards of achieving goals they would never have imagined allows them to recondition, thus retraining the mind so it responds with more courage and confidence to tackle the study.

People who get results more easily are proven to have common beliefs. Research shows that successful "programming" has certain characteristics and reprogramming our thinking model with such beliefs predisposes us to better results. Here are some of the winning beliefs:

"What has been done before can be done again. What one person has done can be done by another. What a person's mind can conceive can be realized."

The most important aspect of each fact is the meaning we attribute to it. Let us learn to attribute a useful and positive meaning to our experiences and erase the negative associations from the past. Nothing happens by chance; in every situation, we can learn something that enriches our lives.

The effort to improve is always worth it. And extraordinary commitment leads to extraordinary results.

It is time to start putting it into practice, but before you whip out the textbooks with your fist of determination clenched, we need to create the ideal conditions, starting with the location, or as I like to call it: The Study Temple.

The Study Temple

Temples are dedicated to sacred activities, a safe space conducive to deep concentration and critical thinking. When you enter a temple, you are enveloped by an atmosphere that impacts your senses and invites you to dedicate yourself to the cause. The place where you study is no different. Incense candles aside, inspiration from positive feelings is just as necessary.

Everyone has a special place where they study in comfort and serenity. What constitutes the perfect place is decidedly different for each person, but in general, it is exclusive to your study. That's why libraries are always full during exam season because they fulfill a single purpose.

If you are someone who uses libraries as a source of distraction and to chat with friends, you're better off staying at home and creating your own study space in private.

Our brain is an expert when it comes to creating habits and associations. If you get used to associating positive emotions with that special study space, you will feel calm and motivated the moment you enter, leading to a more pleasant and smoother experience.

This is why the space we dedicate as our temple should transmit relaxation and tranquility. If we study in a place that causes anxiety or evokes bad memories, the emotional stress will negatively impact effective study. Whereas if we choose a space that always makes us feel calm, our emotions will default to a balanced setting, and we can focus our body and mind on the study.

There are no televisions or cameras or mobiles inside a temple, nothing to distract you from the task at hand because, as expert as the brain is, it can also be quite vague. It can easily succumb to distractions it perceives as easier, more interesting or more emotionally charged than the study, such as a mobile phone or something on the TV.

To avoid temptation, leave any potential distractions outside your temple of study, or at least leave them out of sight. Out of sight, out of mind!

Light:

A good temple must also be well-lit. Lighting influences your mood and affects how you receive and process information.

Light can vary your emotions, making you feel anything from stress and anxiety to tranquility and exaltation, dramatically affecting performance.

Depending on whether you are right- or left-handed, light is also key, especially if you study at night. If you use your right hand, the light must reach you from the left side, opposite to the writing hand. If it's daytime and your table is near a window, natural light should come in from the left side of the text so your arm doesn't create a shadow on your work. This might seem anal, but the brain overexerts when reading the shaded part, and this extra energy could be harnessed for understanding and concentration.

If you do not receive natural light, a portable lamp will suffice, just ensure the whole place is illuminated since a single lamp in full darkness is not a good light source.

If you have a window, not only will you have more natural light, but you can also rest your eyes by looking out at the landscape. After all, the eyes are muscles, and if you constantly force them, it's the equivalent of lifting too much weight at the gym with little pause for rest. You will get too tired, and this is counterproductive. Looking outside for thirty seconds will help you relax your eyes from the strain and recharge before you continue reading.

Position of the text:

Studying with the book resting on the table is useful if you have to underline text or take notes, but the best position for reading is at 45º, so the distance is always the same. If you spend several hours reading and studying during the day, these small measures make a huge difference in the study.

By hand only what is necessary:

The table where you study is not a board game. You do not need hundreds of objects, sheets or books. Clutter leads to disorganization and increases the potential for distraction, which breaks concentration and momentum. Before sitting down to study, decide what you need so you do not have to interrupt yourself to search for tools and resources.

Mobile phones are the biggest culprit, and having it on the table will draw your attention whenever you receive a message or notification. If you do not need to use a computer or tablet, I also recommend removing them from the temple of study for obvious reasons.

Study Cycles

Do you get bored or tired of studying? Does it make you feel sleepy or so exhausted that you can barely turn the page? Study cycles are a technique that solves this problem even for the most difficult subjects.

Some people manage to sit with their head in a book for a whole hour and do no study because they cannot maintain focus on the study. They then tend to devote their time and energy to other more interesting activities.

Some get bored after thirty minutes of study, losing their desire and motivation, and have no choice but to abandon the study altogether.

But there are also people who can sit in front of the text for four hours, exhibiting maximum energy and enthusiasm.

When we sit down to study, we don't consider study durations or scheduled breaks.

Just because you spent four hours with the book open does not mean you have been studying for four hours. You see, there comes a time when your brain needs a break. It is not a machine. At best, you may have maximized your study efforts in the first ninety minutes, but the rest of the time may have been an open-mouthed gaze at the pages with no absorption of the text, meaning the efficiency and quality is different. And therein lies one of the main problems. What is the right amount of time to spend in one study session? How many breaks should one take? How long should those breaks be? How can one avoid wasting precious study time through brain fog due to poor study management? In essence, what kind of schedule will help one master their study time and therefore maximize learning?

The answer is study cycles, and each person, according to their characteristics, must apply a type of cycle.

For those not used to studying:

If studying is not habitual, it doesn't make sense to do a 90-minute study marathon. What you have to do are shorter study cycles.

The first cycle is 25 minutes, followed by a 5-minute pause and then a 5-minute review. Then repeat the 25-5-5 pattern until you reach a maximum of four cycles, equivalent to two hours of study. Studying for 25 minutes instead of 90 will help your mind concentrate all its faculties in a short period without diminishing quality. This will ensure you remain focused for the full 25 minutes without feeling tired or stressed.

For those who want to study without pressure:

If you are used to studying but do not like to spend too much time, the perfect cycle for you involves 45 minutes of study, 10 minutes of pause and 5 minutes for review. You should then repeat this once more. During these 45 minutes, you will study with focus and notice you do not get tired. Furthermore, limiting your study duration using a countdown timer will ensure you dedicate yourself with increased determination, no matter what the study entails. You may be wondering why not just study for an hour straight without breaks. I will explain why it is mandatory to take breaks in the cycles shortly.

Study cycles for perfectionists:

If you are used to spending multiple hours studying without growing tired, the best cycle for you hardcore students is the following:

90 minutes of study, 10-minute pause, 5 minutes for review; 50 minutes of study, 10-minute pause, 5 minutes for review; then 40 minutes of study, 10-minute pause and 5 minutes for review.

You may feel that reducing the second cycle to 50 minutes is unnecessary because you can complete the full 90 minutes, but the truth is your mind begins to lower concentration, decreasing the effectiveness of the study without you realizing it. It is important not to exceed the limit because it implies that your mind has been over-exerting, and therefore functioning at a lesser quality.

Now it's up to you to experiment. Choose the cycle that best suits you, set the stopwatch, and see what happens. If you do not know which one to start with, I recommend you try the 25-5–5 cycle first and work your way up until you tire. This will help you to identify your limits.

Pauses and reviews:

Why are breaks mandatory in study cycles, and how do they benefit your studying?

The breaks are not to rest. It is not the time to lie on your bed or sofa with the phone and slip off into your world. This does not serve to relax your mind and activate you for the next cycle, it only makes your mind disconnect completely, causing you to start over.

The breaks serve to recharge, reactivate and refresh your concentration. For optimal results, get up from the chair and leave the room. Go out on the balcony or outside to breathe in the fresh air. Feel free to take a walk around your house or the library. Go and drink some water, visit the bathroom and eat something like nuts if you're hungry as they give you energy. Avoid sweets, chocolate, cookies or chips as they cause drowsiness and lower your energy levels since your body has to use extra energy to digest them.

During these breaks, do not use your mobile to answer messages or hop onto social networks because they drain cognitive and energy resources.

Why review what you have just studied?

Most students do not spend a few minutes reviewing what they have studied, but it pays to check that you have understood everything or if you have to do a quick revision.

Reviews ensure that information stays in your mind for longer. Review does not mean looking at your notes days or weeks later. That's a waste of time.

After the short break, dedicate your time to reviewing the pages you have read or notes you have taken so far. Recapitulating everything quickly will help your mind assimilate and connect the information with the next.

5 minutes is more than enough: reviewing does not mean studying everything again. Reviewing means looking at the information in a general way, the underlines, titles or keywords so you consolidate and verify that you understand what you have read. It's much simpler than it sounds.

According to the Ebbinghaus oblivion curve, after the first 24/48 hours, we remember only 20% of what we have read in the text. Reviewing the content helps you to raise the curve by refreshing the information in your mind.

Imagine you have to study a 500-page book. You have read and made annotations up until page 300. If, after a week, you return to the first page to review everything, it will be like starting over. If you spend 5 minutes reviewing at the right time, I guarantee you will be able to remember for longer and better understand what you are studying, so you will not have to worry about having to start over and over again from scratch.

At first, you may find it hard to maintain discipline and make the breaks and reviews at specific times, but when you see the results and realize you understand everything better, you are more prepared and stress much less, you will never look back.

Now it's time to apply what you have learned. Use the cycles at least two or three times to discover which one best suits you. Get started right away!

The Master Plan

If you have already experimented with the study cycles, it's time to organize them within a plan, but not just any plan - a Master Plan.

The Master Plan is the ultimate organization tool that ensures you can strike a work-life balance without jeopardizing your studies or sleep and be 100% ready for your next exams. Planning is winning, and this involves factoring in unforeseen events.

It's highly likely you have fixed schedules in your daily life, whether it is classes, extracurricular activities, sports, doctor's appointments or work. What remains of the day is at your disposal. But you won't always be able to plan everything to the finest detail. If you catch the flu and spend two days sick, your routine goes out the window with your soggy handkerchief.

A fundamental principle in the organization is that each task is different and, therefore, you have to learn to treat them differently. For example, studying twenty pages of an easy subject is not the same as studying twenty pages of a complex subject because it does not require the same time or effort.

Grab a piece of paper and a pen. You got them? Okay, let's create a plan to deceive time.

In the first column, write down all your current busy schedules, the fixed activities, and appointments you cannot postpone this entire month, including this week. This should paint a clear picture of the time you need to complete them and what time remains for study and hobbies.

Now, write the subjects you have this semester in the second column. Write how many topics and pages each has so you can know the syllabus' length. You can do this by looking at the index of each subject and highlighting which seem more complicated.

Next, take the weekly agenda that preferably indicates the hours and start placing the fixed activities from the first column.

For the second column, depending on the subject's difficulty, record how many pages you think you can complete in a day. One way to classify the topics is to give them a score of 1 to 10 according to their difficulty level. This will help you determine which topics and subjects require more devotion.

The hours you dedicate to the study will be in conjunction with how many cycles you can do that day. To be realistic, you must know how many pages you can study in a cycle to calculate for the whole day.

Take the 25-minute cycle as an example. For ten pages of a text of difficulty level 2, it is possible to finish them in a cycle of 25 minutes, whereas if it is a text of difficulty level 8, you will need two cycles of 25 minutes (always including pauses and reviews).

If you do this exercise earnestly, you will not be overwhelmed by studying again.

Note in the second column how many cycles you will need for each topic.

Are all topics equally important?

Of course not. Some are merely introductory topics, while others contain the bulk of the entire subject and usually correspond to the last topics of the book.

If you spend too much time, or the same number of hours, studying a topic that is easy to understand that serves as a basis for those who follow it, you will find you need more time to analyze the latest topics with any quality.

For this, you can help yourself with the hints the teacher gives in class (hence the importance of not skipping classes) when they emphasize or highlight certain topic areas or keywords. You can also find out by asking classmates or students from previous years. This is where you have to focus more and label a priority because it's likely to appear in the exam. It's here that you want to achieve 10/10 in terms of quality.

While all the content is important, we cannot aspire to be perfect in all areas, so regarding the topics the teacher does not emphasize, we will aim for a 7 quality rating.

If you have time left at the end of the study, you can always return to the topics that have received less attention. It is better than going over time and missing crucial information. This is why we prioritize, so you have the security of arriving to the exam prepared. If you focus on reaching level 10 quality in all topics, you will know a little about every topic, but nothing in-depth about any.

This technique is perfect for both Global and Analytical learners. If you are Global, you will feel at ease because before commencing, you will see the overall plan that awaits you for the next few days. If you are Analytical, you will feel even the smallest detail is under control.

In Summary

Before setting out on your study journey, you have to create your Master Plan and assemble it by writing the fixed schedules and activities.

Decide which subjects you will study and how many topics there are, see how many pages each topic has and what level of difficulty they entail.

Distribute the cycles in the gaps of the Master Plan, calculating how many serve you to achieve your goal based on the previous point.

We have covered a lot in this chapter, from optimal study cycles to prioritization and the Master Plan. Before we delve into the next chapter regarding reading for speed and efficiency, let's take one of those 5-minute pauses, grab some nuts, a drink, and a breath of fresh air!

Chapter 4
Reading

How can we start reading faster? Saving time in the reading phase while increasing your concentration and comprehension will give you more free time, and you can finish studying feeling satisfied.

In this phase, I will help you raise your level of concentration and explain three things you should always do before you start reading:

1. Prepare your mind to be hyper-focused on reading.
2. How to avoid distractions.
3. How to receive all the new information delivered to your brain.

Preview

Would you like to read twice as fast?

Reading faster does not involve moving your eyes faster, because when you study, you are not only eager to read quickly, but you also need to understand and assimilate the information you are reading at that time. I will teach you techniques to read faster and become more focused and without distraction.

The Trailer Technique

Have you seen the movie trailers before going to the cinema? It provides an insight into the plot, characters, genre, and storyline so you know what to expect.

Books are like movies in that they have introductions, development and an ending, even textbooks. A pity they don't make book trailers for economics or biology!

Normally, the first thing a student does is open the book, choose the topic, and start reading without context. That's like going to the cinema having only read the movie title.

Before you start reading, it's essential that you have seen the trailer. You may not have the cinematographic production of the text, but there is an index in every book that functions similarly.

By viewing the index, you will identify the topics, sections of each chapter, and extensions of each section so your mind is primed to receive the information as it has some idea of what the textbook is about.

Don't forget that your brain is adept at creating associations and needs to know where the collected information in the text comes from and where it goes.

In addition, the brain is inquisitive, and each question is always given an answer. The technique works like this:

Flip through the book and only read the keywords: titles, subtitles, bold words, italics, etc. Ask yourself questions: what will this chapter cover? What is it trying to teach me? What themes and patterns are emerging? Then make a hypothesis about these titles and keywords in the text. What does that word mean to you? What do you think it refers to?

With these questions, you will increase your level of understanding, but you will also be more focused on the text. By fabricating possible hypotheses about the content, your mind will hunt for answers within the text.

When you find the answer to your question, your mind will relish the self-satisfaction of guessing correctly or close enough.

Let's summarize what has happened so far:

- ✓ You have chosen your study cycle.
- ✓ The first 5 minutes are spent flipping through the pages in both the index and the text and making hypotheses about the content.
- ✓ You start reading.

If you've come this far, it's because you want to change something in your studio. Do you still intend to drag your feet on the solution? Go ahead, and you'll see the results will be worth the effort.

How Not to Distract Yourself Again When You Study

List of Distractions

Are you easily distracted by anything? A notification arrives on your screen, and you instinctively look, or your mind wanders away, thinking about what to eat or do later. There is a technique to eliminate distractions, especially those created in your mind, and stay focused when you study.

How does it work?

Actually, it is very simple. Before you delve into your first study cycle, put a blank paper and pencil next to you. Write down the potential distractions that may arise while you study.

Consider this scenario. While studying, your phone rings, and you have several notifications from social networks. Two things can happen: either you fall into temptation, grab your phone and respond accordingly. You are distracted. Or you leave the phone and do not respond, but your mind continues to think about the notifications or missed call, wondering who is contacting you. Again, you are distracted and totally wasting your time.

Prevention is the cure. If you know you are likely to be distracted by your mobile, put it in silence mode and remove it from sight. If you forget, instead of answering every message or call, make a note on the distraction sheet: "call back." And so, with every thought that crosses the mind, whether it is walking the dog, buying batteries or who is cooking tonight, write it down as it comes to mind.

You can include anything, even ideas or thoughts that are not important, like if only I was in Hawaii, how did God make the world in seven days, why do I never have any clean pants?

When your study cycles conclude, you can read through the list, thus identifying two things. On the one hand, you will have a list of pending tasks that need your attention as soon as you have the time. On the other, you will realize the number of meaningless thoughts your mind generates and, therefore, not repeat them in the future.

When you deposit all your thoughts on paper, your brain does not have to divide its attention between essential tasks and studying. Employing this technique, you will be resting your mind and this excess relaxation will help you be more focused.

How to Activate Your Concentration

Concentration is the central axis of any learning process. It is a cognitive process that directs all your mental and operational resources towards an activity or idea.

Study is a cognitive activity, but neither automatic nor mechanical. Therefore, it needs a good dose of concentration so you can carry it out. It is necessary to understand and assimilate complex information and internalize it.

However necessary, it seems that it is impossible to control at times. Sometimes you have it, sometimes you don't. You are neither the first nor the last to have difficulty concentrating. What if you had the power to turn on your concentration? Especially when you have to study those less enjoyable subjects where your mind always tries to escape to a more interesting haven.

You can't always please your mind. If you could, your life would be confined to a couch in front of a television. If you want to achieve your goals, you have to learn to "trick" your mind into doing the things it is striving to avoid. One way to achieve this is by eliminating distractions. You can't fall off the stairs if there are no stairs. And you can't be distracted if there's nothing to distract you.

The Mandarin Technique

No, it does not involve a bowl filled with delicious orange fruit. It is a tried and tested technique that will increase your attention and concentration, making you feel immersed in your study.

To apply this concentration technique, you must use your imagination and follow six steps. Please read them all together carefully and then close your eyes and imagine them without interruption.

1. Close your eyes. Imagine you have a tangerine in your hands. Focus on the details, feeling its consistency, the texture of its skin. Judge its weight. Visualize its color and focus on it. Try to add as many details as possible to this image. Perceive its smell and its temperature, whether it's hot or cold.

2. Imagine you pass the tangerine from one hand to the other.

3. Pass it between your hands, then throw it from one to the other, considering every detail. Try to slow the image down to see it as accurately as possible.

4. Tangerine has a magical power: it can fluctuate in the air. In your mind, leave it in front of you. Move your hands away and watch it float before your eyes. Notice any tiny movements. It is motionless in front of you, suspended in space.

5. The time has come to move the tangerine. Visualize the tangerine rising slowly and imagine it positioned behind your head. Leave it there, floating and fluctuating in the air.

6. Slowly imagine that your visual field is expanding. Try to encompass everything around you. Visualize every detail and appreciate how you feel calmer and more relaxed.

7. Open your eyes, and without breaking this state of concentration, crack on with your studies.

How did it go? Have you managed to concentrate? Regardless of your response on this first attempt, whether positive or negative, focus your attention on these aspects:

- ✓ Relax. There's no rush. Spend a few minutes concentrating.
- ✓ Imagine each step very slowly.
- ✓ Add as many details as possible to the images, they will help you visualize.
- ✓ Get comfortable. Sit comfortably and avoid lying down for this exercise.

At first, it will feel a little mechanical, perhaps you skip a step, but remember that one of the secrets of success is perseverance. In addition, it not only enhances your study, but you can also perform this technique before entering an exam or when you feel nervous and need absolute concentration.

How to Set Goals That Take You Wherever You Want

When a person has a goal in mind, it is much easier to achieve, rather than relying on chance or luck. Most successful people have not gotten there by pure luck, no matter how it seems. Success involves effort and effective organization skills that no one sees.

If your goals are clear and well-marked, they will be easier to achieve. If you sit down to study, you must have a specific purpose or goal. You must have that goal in mind, be it passing an exam, getting the best grade or winning a scholarship.

But it does not serve any objective. It has to be finite, delimited, logical, and technical. The objective is concrete and justified with actions and facts: what you want, what you will do, and how you will do it are the most basic questions that go through your mind when you think about objectives. In this sense, the objectives must be clear and precise, as they determine the direction you are going to take.

I recommend you take some paper and a pencil and list your objectives. I can't emphasize enough how important it is to visualize your goal in writing instead of just thinking about it. In addition, seeing it "outside of you, out of your mind" allows you to make a critical analysis and judgment about what you want to achieve. In most cases, it will lead to a revision of the objective wording and the implications of this in the pursuit of your interests.

Oftentimes, what we think does not fully coincide with what we write, and that should be taken into account because language allows us to think and understand the world around us in the same way it allows us to know ourselves. In fact, it allows you to establish the fundamental bases of your actions.

The objectives have a series of characteristics that serve as a reference to know if your proposed objective is effective for your interests and purposes. In this sense, the objectives have to:

1. **Be specific:** objectives must have the ability to synthesize and specify what you want to achieve. The more specific you are, the better your ability to rate your performance. It is different from saying, "Understand X topic" than "Study five sections." Understanding a topic is too general a term and does not determine the extent to which you could be said to have understood the topic. On the contrary, if your objective is to study five sections of a topic, you can determine your performance in meeting the objective. When there is no confusion about the expected result, it also increases our chances of success as our minds do not wander. It allows us to concentrate better and reduces our anxiety and stress levels.

2. **Be challenging:** Despite being technical goals, they have a subjective load regarding what they represent to you. By this, I mean whether anything challenging will depend entirely on your subjectivity, past experiences, self-confidence, abilities and ambitions. Challenging refers to it being difficult enough to represent a kind of obstacle and we have to deploy all our capabilities and skills to overcome it. It must also be feasible enough for us to realize it. It's illogical if our goal is to do a thirty-kilometer marathon when we don't even train. Nor does it make sense that we propose to run 800 meters if this is well within our capability. To clarify, if it is too difficult, you

will only get frustrated and throw in the towel, but if it is too easy, you will not consider the result as an achievement and will be equally demoralized. If you have high self-confidence, you will perceive the hard-to-achieve goals as challenging rather than impossible. But the same objective can be broken down into micro-objectives, which end up resulting in the same. This means we can fragment and hierarchize a goal into small tasks that are easier to perform. The sum of all these tasks will make us meet the objective.

3. **Have a time limit:** Objectives can't last a lifetime, but they wouldn't be challenging anyway. Give yourself a realistic deadline to fulfill your objective.

4. **Be defined:** Generally speaking, the learning objectives at university are given to us by the teachers. I recommend that you create your own objectives within each subject that align with the subjects. This way, you are convincing your subconscious that you no longer only do it because the teachers tell you to, but that you take responsibility for fulfilling them because you commit to pursuing your objectives.

5. **Getting feedback:** Personal feedback is a gift to yourself that requires honesty about your performance as if you were someone else. As a result, you will find that your performance could have been better if you had given yourself feedback during the process.

The definition of effective objectives is characterized by their formulation considering the what, how, when conditions and what level of implementation they are expected to meet. In addition, there is a fairly basic process for defining objectives that will help you formulate the ones you want and that are useful to you. The steps to follow in this procedure are:

1. **Specify the general objective and tasks to be carried out: This is achieved by answering a question:** what are the most important results you want to achieve in that subject? It is essential to define an objective for each important result we want without overloading ourselves, or you won't know how to organize and achieve everything, drowning in targets.

2. **Specify the expected level of performance:** If your goal is to receive a minimum score of 9 in an exam, your grade will not match your ambitions. If your ideal result is at least 9 and your actual result is 10, you have exceeded your expectation. On the other hand, if your result is 7, there is a two-point gap in your ideal result. In this case (or ideally, in both cases), it is important to review where you fell short. Once you discover the cause, analyze why it happened (you omitted information, did not consider it important, lacked depth) and work towards minimizing the chances of it happening again.

3. **Specify the timeframe:** You do not have to leave your objectives to chance, you have to measure how long it takes to do each task so you can plan objectively. For example, you know how long it takes to read or summarize twenty pages.

4. **Prioritize objectives:** It consists of selecting and hierarchizing the most important objectives. To know how to prioritize, we have to take into account the degree of urgency to achieve it and its level of importance.

Not everything is technical, but the objectives have a great motivational component:

1. **The relevance of the goal:** why you have chosen that objective is your biggest motivator and will lead you to the end, but you cannot forget to remind yourself every day. You can write it on the agenda, on a post-it note in the room or set the alarm on your mobile as a reminder.

2. **Use rewards:** Every time you do something that brings you closer to achieving your objective or micro-objectives, reward yourself with a small prize. It can be your favorite food, a movie, or treat yourself to a gift.

3. **Convince yourself of your abilities:** This increases the probability of your subconscious seeing the objective as something realistic and tangible because it is appropriately challenging.

How to Read Twice as Fast to Have Twice as Much Free Time

Have you ever started reading a text and realized you had not absorbed anything?

This happens because of distractions. Imagine you are reading and come across the word Italy. At that moment, your brain disconnects from the text to think about the wonderful holiday you spent in Genoa.

Our brains are constantly distracted. You know why? Because the brain has two hemispheres. The right side is the rational hemisphere and the left is the creative hemisphere. When we read, we activate the rational part of our brains while distractions occur due to the creative hemisphere. When you study, there is a constant struggle between both hemispheres, and each one gives priority to the most interesting information.

With strategic reading, we can take advantage of the corpus callosum, a structure that connects the hemispheres coordinating both functions so they can join forces and help you achieve your objectives. Consequently, distractions while reading are eliminated, concentration is maintained, and reading speed improves.

The pointer technique will help you achieve this result.

People believe it is normal to read from left to right with a fluid movement. After all, that is what we are taught in school. The truth is that our eye does not make a linear path along the lines, rather it creates points of fixation in each word, hopping from word to word instead of reading the entire sentence in a single fluid glance.

It is true that the eye moves from left to right when reading Latin languages, but not fluidly as if following a line, which creates leisurely reading. Do the test: record yourself reading a paragraph and you will notice your eyes are constantly stopping.

We have been taught to read like this. First, we learned to put the letters together in syllables, then create words, then form sentences. This way of reading involves a fractured process that slows your reading ability. Keep in mind that the eyes are a muscle, and like any muscle, it can be trained to be faster and stronger. When we start running as a hobby or to train for an event, our legs carry us for perhaps only a kilometer until one day, we reach ten kilometers with ease. The same thing happens with our eyes. Moreover, we have been taught to read using the rhythm of the tongue, a much slower muscle than the eyes. In fact, when you read, you have probably heard that little voice repeating every word in your mind. Think about how long it takes to pronounce the word "computer" and how long it takes your eyes to see that word. It's not about talking faster but using your eyes' potential to learn faster.

To stop wasting time and effort with each fixation, you have to re-learn to read. You already know how to read, otherwise you wouldn't be here, reading this paragraph on this page, but you do not read at the optimal speed. You have to change the way you look at the sheet, letters, words and sentences to read fluidly.

The Pointer Technique

You need a pencil or pen for this. Place the tip under the line you are going to read and move it in a smooth, fluid motion with a consistent speed that suits you, ensuring that you understand what you are reading. Try to follow the rhythm of the pencil or pen tip so that it guides the eyes rather than vice versa.

Redo the test: record yourself reading using this technique. Do you notice the difference? The eye follows a linear path instead of stopping at each word. Practice it a few times before your next study cycle so you find a speed that allows you to understand and advance simultaneously.

Now that you have found your ideal reading speed, let's put it into practice and get studying. Before you do, make sure you complete the trailer technique. Remember this is a practical book, so there is no better time to start testing what we have learned than right now. So set the number of pages you want to study as a goal, reset the stopwatch with the study cycle duration you have chosen and use the trailer technique, then grab a pencil or pen and start reading using the pointer technique.

When you're done, answer these questions:

- ✓ How many pages have you read?
- ✓ With what level of quality did you perceive what you studied? Score it between 0 and 10

List all your distractions.

____

____

____

____

____

Having made some adjustments to your way of reading and studying, you have already achieved a change, and we are only at the beginning of the method! Congratulations! During the study cycle, did you feel more energetic, awake and engaged compared to before?

I bet you were more focused. Concentration is one of the most influential factors when studying because productivity depends on it. As a result, we not only improve speed but, above all, concentration, since using the pointer does not give the mind time to deviate from its objective.

It is like driving a car on a straight road at 20km per hour. By moving slowly, we can play music, talk to our passengers, daydream or look at the landscape. But when we step on the accelerator and travel at 200km per hour, we can no longer afford those distractions as they imperil our lives and risk us not reaching our target destination.

In summary, reading slowly leaves us vulnerable to distraction whereas reading fast maximizes concentration.

Reading fast is one thing, comprehending it is another. That is what we will look at in the next chapter.

Chapter 5
Comprehension

"I don't understand anything." Does this phrase ring true for you? Many students experience this when studying, forcing them to go through every page until everything is clear before moving forward.

Information goes through a series of phases: coding, the means by which information is recorded, and storage, where our brain saves and retrieves information. To grasp a solid understanding, it is necessary to learn how to enhance these phases.

You are Not Dumb

We've all been called dumb at least once or labeled incapable of achieving something. Out of all those voices, yours may stand out the most.

Let's do a little test - quickly read the following text carefully:

The procedure is very simple. First, we place things in various groups. Obviously, each tower is created based on the different characteristics of the elements. An error when selecting the elements could irreparably damage all the elements in a group, so the selection phase is really important. If you do not have all the necessary material to start the procedure, it is necessary to find what is missing, otherwise you cannot move on to the next phase. It is important not to accumulate too many elements to avoid an overload, but this is a general rule that you can apply in life, not only during this process. Naturally, different groups should be treated with different modalities, but in general, the procedure is the same. Once the different phases of the process are concluded, the elements are different groups that move to the final procedure and put them in place for use according to the need, then use, and finally repeat the entire procedure.

Did you understand anything?

No? Don't worry, that's totally normal because you're missing one critical element - the context. You do not have a point of reference or any details, so the text makes little sense. We can determine that a process must be followed and some elements cannot be missed, but what is it about? Now I will give you the context, in this case, the article title.

DOING LAUNDRY.

Now you have the context, re-read the text and you will see how much easier it is.

The procedure is very simple. First, we place things in various groups. Obviously, each tower is created based on the different characteristics of the elements. An error when selecting the elements could irreparably damage all the elements in a group, so the selection phase is really important. If you do not have all the necessary material to start the procedure, it is necessary to find what is missing, otherwise you cannot move on to the next phase. It is important not to accumulate too many elements to avoid an overload, but this is a general rule that you can apply in life, not only during this process. Naturally, different groups should be treated with different modalities, but in general the procedure is the same. Once the different phases of the process are concluded, the elements are different groups that move to the final procedure and put them in place for use according to the need, then the use, and finally repeat the entire procedure.

The problem is not your ability or your intelligence, rather the text is not providing you with enough information to understand it.

The preview provides a context of what you are going to read. If you start your study cycles without having done the preview, you will lack context, like with the laundry procedure, making you feel defeated. It's not a matter of capacity but having all the information you need.

Would you like to understand even the most difficult topics? I can show you how to make sure no text can evade you.

Let's look at the techniques you have to apply to increase your understanding.

Techniques to Understand Everything

1. Short Film

Remember we talked about the preview as a trailer? Now this trailer will turn into a short film due to this next technique, which is especially useful for people with the ANALYTICAL cognitive style, so pay attention if this is you.

Let's say you are in front of a text but cannot understand it well for whatever reason.

What should you do? The answer is simple. Flip through the text and, in addition to reading the titles and subtitles, read the first and last paragraphs of each topic section. This is a brief immersion into the text before you start reading in-depth, improving your overall hypothesis.

This will provide you with a mental photograph of the text, and you can discover what the sections are about. It may seem that you are doing more work and wasting time, but in reality, you are saving it. If you read from the beginning without understanding anything, you will have to re-read it. With this technique, you won't.

To considerably improve with a complex text, it is best to add this after the preview. Because if you are reading a text you do not understand and move on, you won't understand anything the text tries to tell you. Books are progressive, and each chapter is tied to the last. It's like starting a movie thirty minutes in. You have no idea what has happened in the movie until now, so nothing makes sense.

Creating a decent knowledge foundation of the book will be much easier to understand as you progress.

Still struggling? Still unclear of the book's contents or your teacher's lectures?

Don't fear, there is another technique to improve your level of understanding. It is called the compass.

2. The Compass

Often within a text, there is a single word you do not understand, either because you do not know it or understand its context. The unknown term then begins to unravel the text, and you lose your way.

This usually happens with extremely technical subjects that have industry-specific words, especially difficult for first-semester students. There is a solution.

The compass technique works similarly to a real compass, ensuring you do not lose your way. Before your class even begins, you have to spend some time looking at the subject.

In this case, there are two elements that serve as your compass:

- ✓ **The syllabus**, providing a snapshot of the topics and contents you will learn.
- ✓ **The glossary** of specific terms as they allow you to find your way when lost within the text due to an unknown word.

When you feel stumped because a word throws out the meaning of the entire text, look for a glossary specific to that subject and find the meaning of the word. Then re-read the text and fill in the gaps.

3. The Return of the Dictionary

I'm going to introduce you to your new best friend: the dictionary. It can be digital or physical, and you will use this old-fashioned yet timeless tool.

Having the dictionary at hand will assist you with any difficult, technical words when they arise.

Every word you do not understand leads to temporary confusion or a gap in comprehension, so look it up in the dictionary. It does not matter if you take a little longer in your cycles, the important thing is you understand the text in depth, setting you on the path to success.

4. The YouTube Technique

YouTube is not just a time-wasting device. It is an ocean of audio-visual information where you can find experts in various fields, including yours.

From CEOs to teachers uploading explainer videos, you can find almost anything on YouTube. It's the ultimate search engine. Whenever you lack understanding of a subject, call on YouTube and search using the keywords.

It's an interactive study method with your personal teacher and industry expert explaining everything you need to know and more.

5. The Importance of Creativity

Creativity plays a decisive role in intelligence; it helps you create new brain connections thanks to partnerships and the creation of surprising solutions. When you let your creative juices flow, all manner of ideas and innovations materialize. How can you enhance your creativity?

6. Brainstorming

This technique came from advertising, where creating innovative and eye-catching ideas to promote products or services is the key to success.

To begin with, you must think about a problem that is not really a problem. It is important to think about this "problem" as something that does not affect you since it is always easier to look for solutions to problems unrelated to us. This way, we have no emotional ties and are less likely to make irrational decisions or come up with hair-brained ideas. One problem might be "how to earn a million dollars in ten minutes."

The second phase consists of finding solutions to that problem and recording them. To do this well, there are rules:

- ✓ Zero criticism: never judge the suggested solutions. All are valid, no matter how "out there" they may seem.
- ✓ Quality vs. quantity: the important thing is to point out as many solutions as possible, even if they lack quality.

You'll need to create ten solutions to this single problem every day for thirty days, or thirty solutions every day for ten days. **Thus, reaching 300 solutions for a single problem.**

I warn you that the first 100 will be the easiest because your mind is fresh and will conjure up common solutions. But it will gradually become more difficult until you think, "I don't know what else to write anymore." That is when the exercise is really starting. It is at this moment when you find yourself desperate, drawing blanks, fighting through mind fog, scraping at the base of your brain when it comes to life, creating new connections and associations, called lateral thinking, involving thinking "outside the box" or outside the patterns to which we are accustomed, as one of the characteristics to be able to develop lateral thinking is to run out of options.

7. Image Streaming

This technique is more advanced and improves your intellectual capacity. The creator of this technique was Richard Poe in his book "The Einstein factor" where he explains how this impacts your brain capacity.

It is important to practice this technique at least 15 minutes a day, preferably before going to sleep, as this is the best time.

First, close your eyes and let your imagination loose. Images, colors, words, rest assured something will appear. Then describe it in detail, including the colors, shapes, how it smells, its texture, if there are sounds.

Imagine this image in a meadow with animals and a tree. You approach the tree and begin to describe everything you see, hear and feel. The images then change, the tree transforms into something else, and whenever something changes, describe what you see. Best to do this over 15-20 days. If you have someone to give you feedback, even better, because random images sometimes take on new meaning through connections and interactions.

For example, one of the stories Richard Poe tells is of a boy who begins his first sessions during his course. A person comes to describe the wheel of his girlfriend's car, and, while describing it, has a bad feeling. Richard, upon hearing this, is intrigued and asks the boy to call the girlfriend. To their surprise, they learn that the car wheel had a problem. When taking her to check, they discover it could have exploded at any time due to the damage.

Richard Poe says this information is held by your brain from things you've seen but not on a conscious level.

According to Poe, this boy saw something that did not quite fit while getting out of the car but did not pay attention to it, so his memory came from his subconscious.

This technique not only allows you to recall important information or details but also to create new neural connections through the process of searching and describing the images that appear and transforming them. Thanks to this, a part of your normally inactive brain will be activated.

It's a quick exercise, and when you do it, you will notice the results in no time. From the first month, you will be able to measure the differences, react faster, and function at an intellectual level far better.

If you do not have someone to give you feedback on the images, record yourself in audio and listen to it later. Another important factor involves closing your eyes so as not to notice anything around you that might contaminate the images, as it can interrupt the whole process. Try staring into the lightbulb and then closing your eyes as the light will take certain forms in your mind, and you can describe from there.

To recap, we can apply various techniques to ensure we never have to say "I don't understand anything" ever again. You've seen the trailer and now you're ready to watch the short film. YouTube and the dictionary are your new best friends, so difficult, technical words are no longer an issue. And now you know how to activate your brain and get your creative juices flowing like Victoria Falls. So, how does this make us more organized? Let's find out!

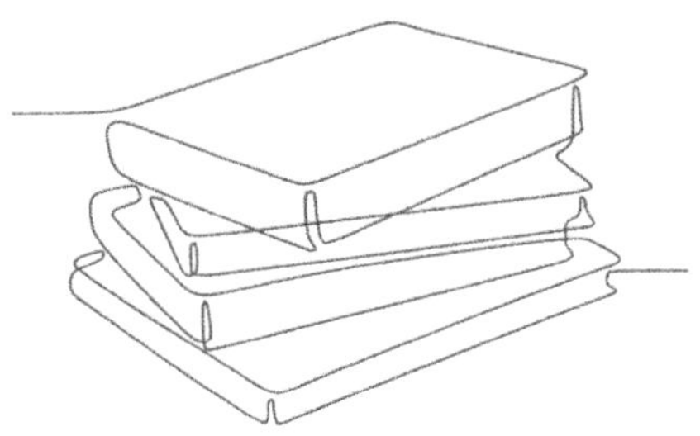

Chapter 6
Organization

The time has come for me to explain what you should do before, during and after studying your textbooks.

I will explain three things in detail:

1. How to select important information.
2. How to make an outline or summary.
3. How to take perfect notes.

A New Way to Study

Let's talk about the organization's first and most important phase - reading for comprehension, determining what is important, how to extract and then synthesize it.

1. Underlining is Out of Fashion

Underlining is tempting, especially when reading something complicated or incomprehensible. When you underline it, you believe you will read it again later and understand it, tricking yourself into thinking this is good study. But you and I know this is just an illusion.

There is a way to avoid filling the textbook with meaningless fluorescent colors and underlines. They are the keywords and the technical details.

2.   The Importance of Keywords

Keywords summarize an entire concept and are extremely subjective since they do not have to be implicit in the text. However, after reading the concept, you can create a word that reminds you of what it means in the book.

The huge difference between keywords and underlining is they force you to understand what you are studying and summarize it in one or a few keywords. You can't just underline random words, but having understood the paragraph or heading, you'll have to figure out what word or set of words to summarize what you just read.

This makes many, especially perfectionists and those who habitually underline the whole book, feel skeptical about this technique. They believe it is impossible to summarize a concept in a single word or that details would be lost along the way.

But let's not get ahead of ourselves. I still have to explain the technical details.

Technical details are objective pieces of information that cannot be summarized like personal names, dates and addresses. Features are also technical details. This type of information provides more depth and accuracy in your learning and gives your teacher a nice surprise during exams.

3. Verification

Now that you have identified the technical details, you have to organize it. But first, we need to verify it. This important phase is called, you got it, verification.

Verification is necessary for checking the keywords and technical details you have selected are correct, that when reading them, you remember why you had selected them, and check if something is missing or repeated.

It's possible that:

- ✓ Everything works perfectly, and you remember the concepts with the keywords and technical details you need.
- ✓ You realize you have skipped a concept and must add more keywords. It may also be that there are two keywords for the same concept, and you must eliminate one.
- ✓ You realize the keyword you have chosen is not the right one as it does not represent the concept you want to evoke, so you look for the next keyword for that concept.

The perfect time to do the verification is when reviewing the study cycle.

Once your words and details are ready, what do you do with them? An outline? A summary? Neither! You will do a mind map.

Mind Maps

With the keywords and technical details already selected, it is time to arrange them in a mind map, the perfect place to organize the information from the text. Now I want to show you a map I call the "map of maps" that will show you all the features a mind map should have. Best of all, this map is composed of keywords and details.

As you can see, the map's central core is where all the arguments begin. Sprouting from the core is the branch to write the keyword, a drawing, and a series of words to complement the main keyword.

- ✓ The sheet must be horizontal.
- ✓ The branches stem from the title, following the hands of the clock.
- ✓ Write everything in CAPITAL LETTERS. This will make it easier to make revisions as the eye perceives them quicker and more efficiently.
- ✓ The rings follow: this is a way of dividing the themes and subtopics on the same branch. Each branch must have a main ring where most of that topic is condensed, however, as seen in the example above, a subtopic may arise from a keyword that must be specified, this is when another ring arises. This is well exemplified in the part where it says VISUAL. This second ring comes from the CREATION branch, and is necessary to clarify this word as it cannot be done in the branch or main ring.
- ✓ Visual drawings are important, since it activates visual memory. It's easier to remember a picture than a word, and images help us remember concepts. You can make a drawing for each branch or ring that is difficult to remember. It does not matter if your drawing skills are subpar, it can be something simple.

✓ Colors are also important to help memory and to create associations between concepts. Related items can be the same color.

One of the biggest advantages of a mind map is the need to understand the subject deeply, otherwise you will not be able to produce it. This leads to higher quality, unlike summaries or underlining, often leading to self-deception about understanding the text.

How do we study or memorize the mind map in the best way? To answer this effectively, I have two tips:

1. Do not overload the space. Be economical with the amount of information used on the map. Remember that keywords are subjective and will not serve others and vice versa.
2. Make the mind map after you've done the verification of your keywords and technical details. Don't rush before you have this clear, as it can backfire. You may be forced to make more than one map when you realize you need to make corrections.

Transform your notes in class

We have come this far, explaining what a mind map is, how to create one, and its purpose. Now for some tips to become an expert using the notes you take in class. When at home with your book, you can go at your own pace, but the teacher dictates the rhythm in a classroom.

During class, people take notes differently:

✓ **Those who listen without taking notes.** The advantage, without a doubt, is a greater understanding of the contents and a strong grasp of the subject. Reluctant or even rebellious students who take no notes normally settle for a mediocre result. On the other hand, it may be that the student is ambitious, confident, and therefore convinced they will remember everything once the subject's central concept has been understood. It is a choice that saves paper and encourages class interaction. It also comes with disadvantages. The first is that this information, as we saw with the curve of oblivion, will not remain there forever, and after a couple of hours you will have forgotten a lot. The second is that it is much easier to get distracted and lose the teacher's thread.

✓ **Those who point to the last comma of what the teacher says.** The advantage is that you can review the class content at home. These people usually need to have everything under control, but it has a great disadvantage; you are not fully present in the class since you are too concentrated scoring, and incomplete notes are the equivalent of useless notes, especially if you have not heard or understood the concepts that were explained while taking them.

✓ **Those who listen and understand class content and only then take notes.** The advantage is you manage to understand everything in class. The disadvantage is that while you are frantically writing to catch up with your peers, the teacher continues to talk, but you are too busy writing to catch anything.

Notes are better than any treasure map. Here's why:

1. They record only the keywords and do not evidence concepts or entire phrases. The acquired synthesis capacity means you gain time and concentration.

2. They promote active learning. To choose a keyword, you have to listen (or read) to understand.

3. They help you stay focused. When you're focused on organizing information, there's no way to distract yourself.

4. They give you a complete overview of what is spoken in the classroom. If it is Global, you will greatly appreciate it. While at home, you will no longer have the unpleasant feeling of wondering if you have missed something in class.
5. They allow you to memorize in the long run. Well-crafted notes are a guarantee of long-term results.
6. They are easy to review. The advantage of having a global vision is that it provides an opportunity to review a plethora of information in a few minutes.
7. They can be enriched, meaning arrows, post-its or boxes to decorate your notes are relegated to history.
8. They help you prioritize topics. A good trick to understanding the arguments the teacher highlights is to divide the sheet of paper into four parts before starting the class. At the end, observing the amount of information noted in each section will demonstrate how much time has been dedicated, indicating that it is the most important.
9. They give order and clarity. Very clear notes on paper mean clear data in the mind.
10. They set you apart from others. They tend to generate much curiosity and can become a topic of conversation, even with the teacher.

Remember, it's important to remember that whatever the keyword, it's what it evokes in you as they are extremely personal.

Here are some mind maps that can inspire you to start creating your own.

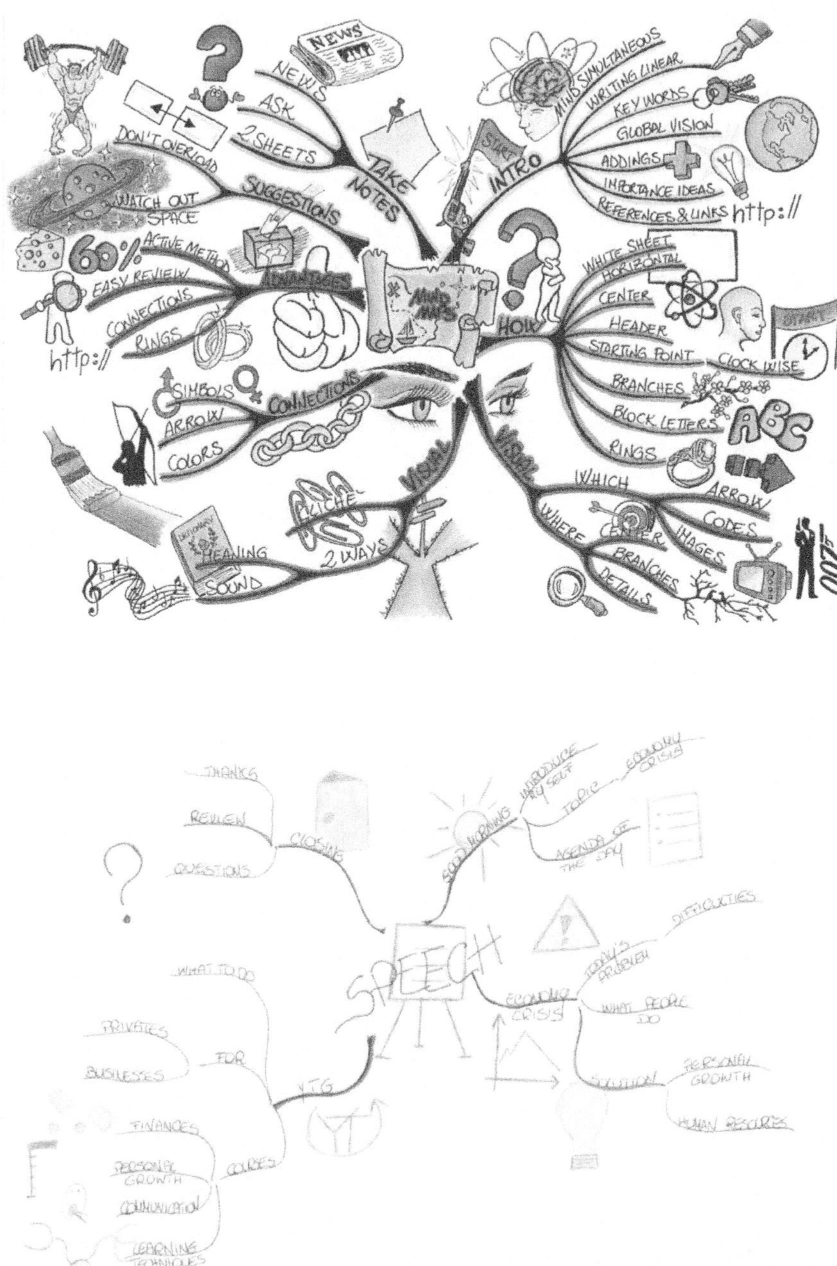

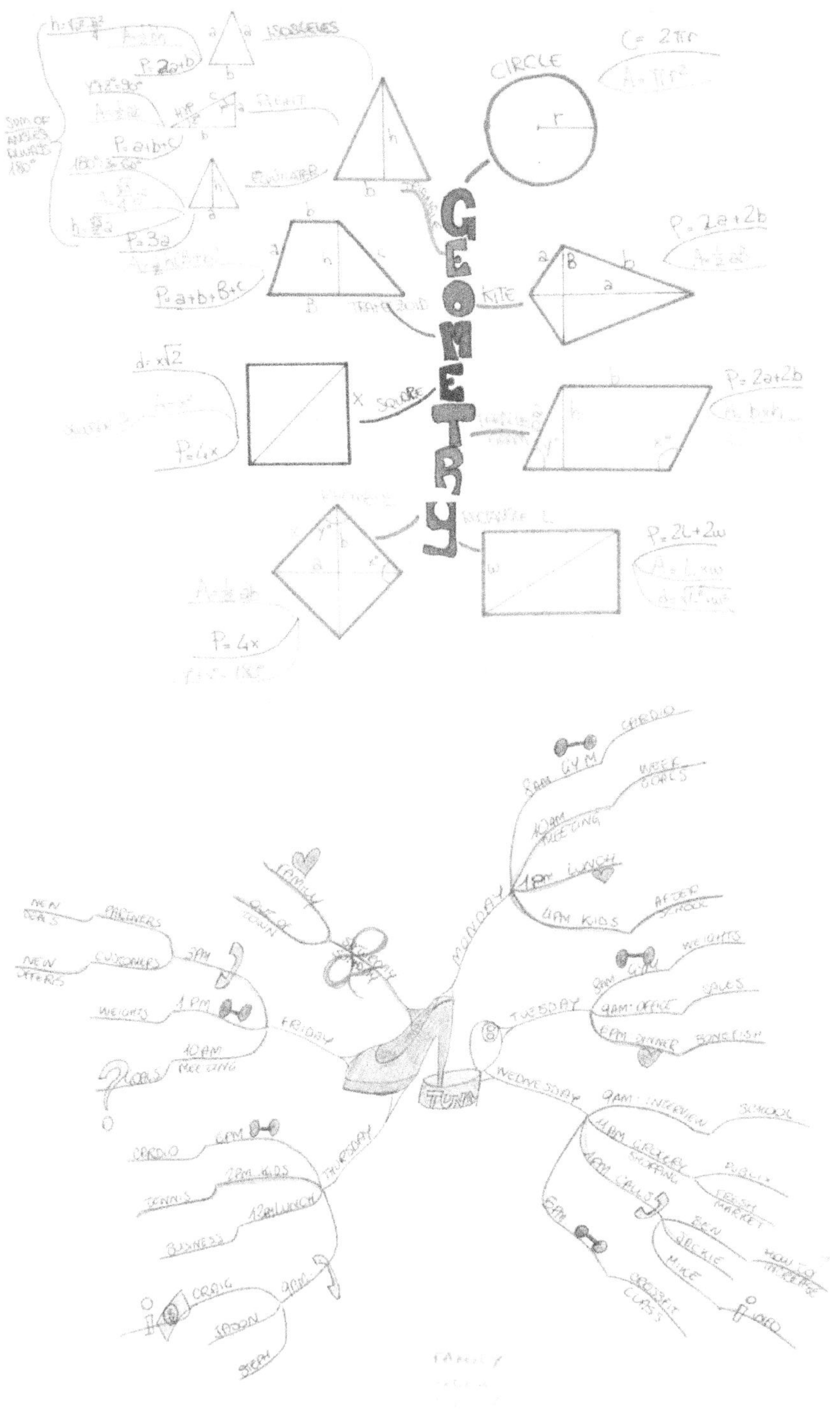

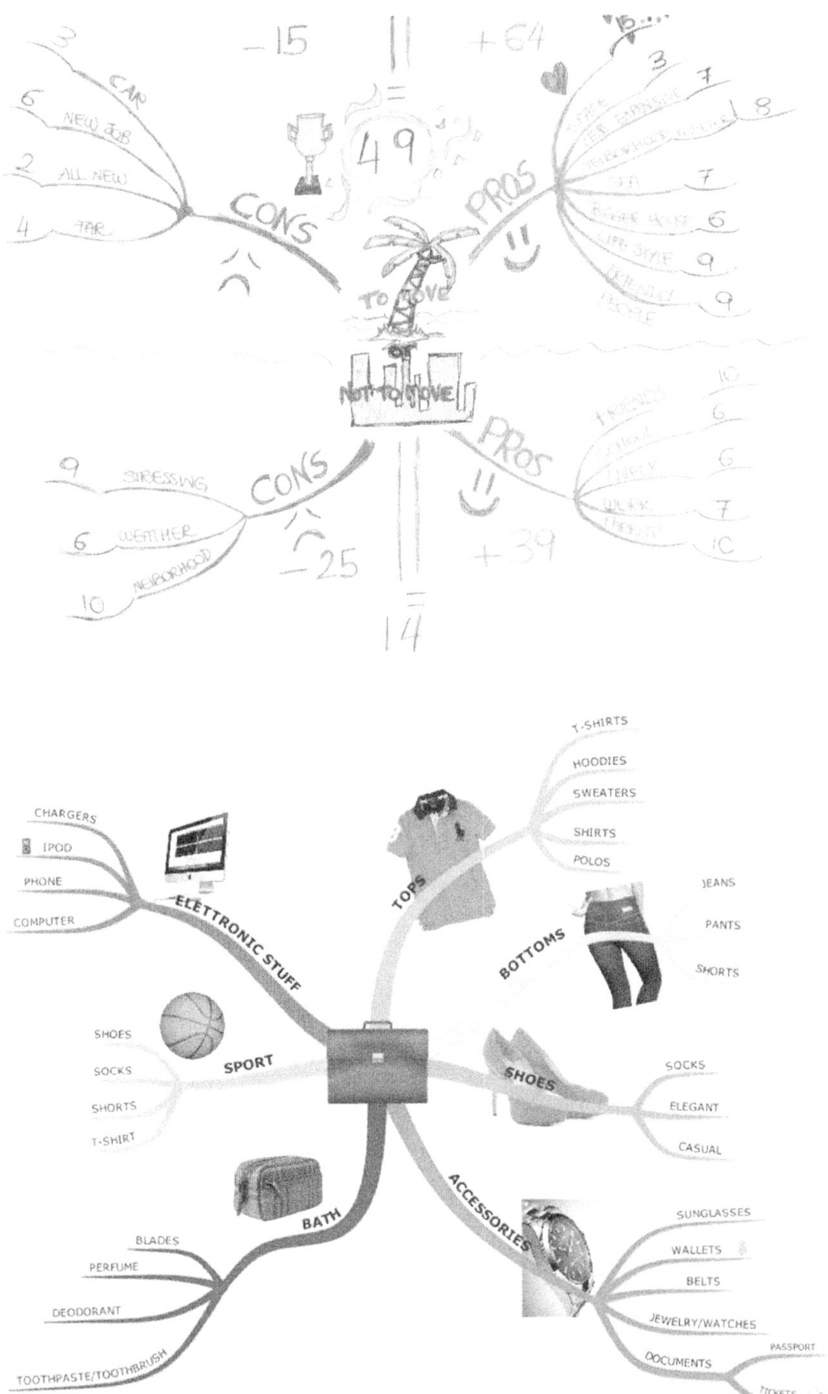

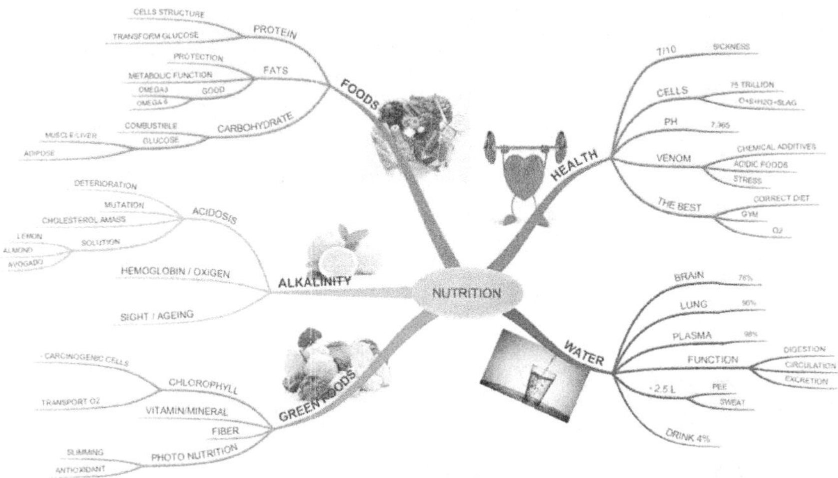

Organizing your notes effectively will ensure you never miss a keyword or key concept. Notebooks and tablets are perfect note-taking devices, but one note-taker trumps all else – the mind! Once you master the art of memorization, the ultimate thesaurus will remain shelved inside your head forever. It's time to learn how!

Chapter 7
The Memory

We have arrived at the most critical and perhaps most hated reading skill: memorization. People normally memorize information by reading and repeating, but some read, write, then re-read, repeating this cycle until the content has been learned by rote. For example, what do you do when you are learning a foreign language? Repeat it several times, or write it down, and repeat until mastered. This technique has several limitations:

- ✓ Reading and writing is an arduous process and takes a long time to memorize.
- ✓ It is extremely boring.
- ✓ The content is forgotten in the long term as it only works if used shortly after memorization, whether a few days or weeks.
- ✓ What you memorize will stay in your mind for no longer than a month.

In the forgetting curve of Ebbinghaus, it is said that the amount of information contained in the mind that can be regurgitated between

24 and 48 hours is 23% to what you have seen. Put another way, approximately 80% of the information memorized is lost after just two days.

That is why my goal with this chapter is to share some memorization techniques that help you retain the information for much longer than two days.

Memory is linked to memorization. I will teach you how to retain information quickly and effectively without having to go through painstaking repetition, avoiding parrot-fashion speak.

You don't need to behave like a trained robot, but people who understand and rework the studied information make it their own. From this point of view, memorization is not an end but an instrument that allows you to expand and retain gained knowledge.

I will teach you memory techniques that integrate seamlessly with previous learning strategies.

The time has come for you to really commit yourself and apply everything I teach you because doing the minimum to pass no longer works. With your newly acquired techniques, you can revolutionize your way of studying and your academic journey.

The Secret Formula of Memory

This formula has three elements that you must know to improve your memory.

$$\text{Memory} = (\text{emotion} \times \text{frequency}) / \text{time}.$$

What does this mean?

The ability to memorize information is directly proportional to the emotions that said information evokes in us and the frequency with which that information is repeated. It is inversely proportional to the time spent learning the information, from beginning to end.

Let me simplify in case you are lost: If you want to memorize something, you have to feel strong emotions, repeat the experience several times and do it over a specific period.

The Power of Emotions

Have you ever wondered why you remember some things that are not important and forget others that are? You remember the smallest detail of your first kiss but forget where you left your passport. You get chills whenever you think about your bike accident when you were little, but forget the name of the person in charge of your interview. Well, the ones you remember are linked to emotions. You see, positive and negative emotions are imprinted in our memory.

You may find this interesting but think the only emotions your boring subjects stir up are ones of despair.

Generally, we have difficulty memorizing because we create no emotional relationship with what we are studying. It's not easy to get excited about a molecular biology thesis or a law textbook, but with the techniques you've learned so far, if they haven't been enough to interest you in the study, you'll perhaps find these memorization techniques comical.

The Importance of Frequency

As observed, emotions are not enough to create a robust memory so we will talk about how frequently you make contact with the information.

It's what advertisers do; they bombard you with ads until you're unconsciously choosing their brand in the supermarket. It's a subtle form of brainwashing.

How can you use this to your advantage when you study? You have to apply the efficient and effective "repetition protocol." Repeating obsessively in a short time is not the way to go, so night marathons before an exam are pointless.

When memorizing is a matter of time

Time is not something you can ignore. The more times you see the study material in a short period, the more effective it will be.

With the Master Plan, you can organize your time by concentrating on one subject for as much as possible. Jumping from one subject to another too often is ineffective.

Let's start delving into memory techniques.

Remember With Emotion

Emotional or implicit memory represents the oldest form of long-term memory that exists. Instinctive reactions, which have played a fundamental role in the evolution of our species, have remained in this part of our memories.

From the anatomical point of view, emotional memory is located in the amygdala, a part of the brain that receives stimuli from both internal and external factors, giving it emotional meaning. It is also responsible for implicit learning, which can be created with chromatic variations, voice tone, and movement rhythm.

How can you activate it if you have to memorize 500 pages of content?

The techniques presented below have been designed to stimulate the amygdala so the information rises in the most primitive part of your brain. I will teach you three techniques of emotional memorization. For each one, I will indicate the cognitive style for which it is most suitable. It is important to underline that emotional memorization is effective in remembering either concrete or abstract concepts and instructions.

1. The Puzzle Technique

If your cognitive style is predominantly VISUAL, you have to use visual structure, chromatic variation, and images to stimulate your emotional memory.

This technique is based particularly on the use of mind maps, which are effective for reviewing for an exam.

Here is the strategy to put it into practice:

Make one or multiple mind maps of the method phases we have seen so far, from Approach to Organization.

Now take one of the maps you have made and put it aside because you will voice everything you remember from that chapter, following the structure of the created mind map.

Even if you don't remember many details and it's not entirely accurate, strive to recall as much information as possible. This mental "effort" will further reinforce the neural connections created during the reading and making of the map.

Fill in the missing holes by looking at the chapter inside the book and stopping to read the parts that are not yet clear more carefully.

After processing each map, it is time to do the final review, where you will memorize all the concepts forever.

Put all the maps on the ground next to each other, arranging them so that all those related are together, creating a great puzzle. Building this mind map puzzle will help you create new neural networks in your mind and associate information more quickly.

Stand in front of your super map, close your eyes and breathe deeply for thirty seconds, then open your eyes. What was the map you saw first? Read it out loud. When you finish, move on to the next map until you've read them all.

I assure you that seeing the entire exam mapped out on the floor will impact your emotional memory, and you will remember the information by its position on the floor during the exam.

Emotional memorization for a stylish person global-verbal (GLOVER) consists of repeating as if you were a grandparent.

In this case, you describe what you are studying in simpler terms as if you had to explain it to your grandparent. If you understand, it means you have assimilated and internalized what you have studied.

I also advise you to repeat some definitions with a strange accent, as this will make you feel so ridiculous that it will influence your emotional memory.

2. Theatrical Presentation

If your style is visual-analytical (VISANA), this is your technique. This strategy consists of creating a theater performance, even if your acting skills need polishing. You can use this technique after you have made the chapter map or in the review phase of the puzzle technique.

In this case, you have to repeat the information using your physique as if a performer in a play: accentuate your facial expression, stand up, move around the room, and gesticulate when you speak.

Remember that emotional memory works in such a way that any image generates a reaction at the neurophysiological level, such as, for example, an increased heart rate.

3. Tales and Other Stories

This technique works for VERANA (verbal-analytical) and VISANA.

Memorizing is useless if you have not understood what you are studying. But there are exams where you cannot afford the slightest mistake, so I will teach you how to also memorize formulas, very specific information but at the same time abstract.

For this, I advise you to build stories as in the following case.

Take a theorem or a formula and associate each component with a character in a story using as much fantasy as you can muster.

Invent a story with these characters as protagonists depending on the order and mathematical relationship the components of the formula have.

You will see it clearer with an example. Suppose this invented formula: $2n + 5s = 0$

The symbol "n" can be a dwarf and the symbol "s" can be a snake, then you imagine two dwarfs dancing with five snakes. It's an absurd story, but the more absurd it is, the easier it will be to remember.

Memory and Frequency

The more times you see information and the more you repeat it, the more familiar it will become. I'm not talking about the classic mechanical repetition that you have become accustomed to since you were a child, but a repetition protocol so that the neural networks of information are reinforced in your mind.

This technique works great when you have to remember a lot of data, like dates and articles.

Give the play to the mental recorder.

This technique can be integrated into anyone's study method and preparation for any exam. You can use it before reading a chapter or studying a mind map.

It consists of:

- ✓ A mental review sequence that helps you vary study sessions to make you less bored.
- ✓ It also consists of a mantra that turns on your mental recorder through a high-impact visualization.

Sequential Mental Review

Long-term recall is not difficult if you apply a mental review technique:

- ✓ You can do it during the 5-minute review of the study cycle.
- ✓ At the end of the day, before going to sleep, review the arguments you have studied or the mind map for 10 minutes.
- ✓ After three days, do a final review of your studied material for no more than 15 minutes.

As we have already seen in the forgetting curve, this sequence guarantees you the maximum memorization percentage of information with minimum effort.

The Mantra

The brain is like a recorder, but if you don't press the REC button, nothing will be recorded.

Oftentimes, all you need to improve memory is to simply be aware that we can remember things, so before each review, repeat this mantra:

- ✓ **Believe it**: convince yourself you will remember what you are going to study.
- ✓ **Wish it**: make yourself want more than ever to remember what you are studying.
- ✓ **Visualize it**: repeat information aloud clearly.
- ✓ Ask for it: instruct your brain to remember what it is studying.
- ✓ **Review it**: look at the material one last time.

It may seem silly but if you try it, you will never return to your old study habits.

1. Delayed Repetition and the Flashcard Method

I want to reassure you that the goal of this book is not to have you repeat text like a parrot. Numerous studies have shown that memorization improves when we are exposed to the same information distributed over an extended period.

If you have to learn new language vocabulary, rules and laws or industry jargon, such as medical school, you have to use evenly spread repetition by applying the flashcards method.

Take a post-it note or piece of card, or use Quizlet or AnkiApp.

Write the name of the virus or what you need to learn on the front. I also recommend you draw it.

Write the definition or characteristics that you have learned on the back.

Mix them all, pick one at random and try guessing the definition from the name of the virus or vice versa.

Schedule reviews after two days, four days, ten days and so on until exam day.

2. Become the Author of Your Audiobook

For GLOVER AND VERANA students who study and work, perhaps spending a lot of time driving or riding public transport, audiobooks are the way to go. Audiobooks have a huge advantage; you can take them with you wherever you go and listen to them anytime, any place. Of course, not all university books come with audio, but so many do.

The next time you study, record yourself with your mobile while doing the mind map. This first repetition can be detailed so you don't have to return to the book. Then listen to the recording while shopping, walking, or riding the subway.

You may be easily distracted the first time around and lose the thread, so persevering will improve and reinforce your concentration, training your memory. Just be careful while driving.

Memorize Lots in a Short Time

So far, I have taught you techniques specific to university students. Combined with the techniques explored in previous chapters, it should lead you to obtain the results you're after.

Now I will teach you the classic mnemonics used in memory championships. These techniques are powerful and enable you to memorize a huge amount of information quickly, so I have left it for later.

Playing With the Images

Visual is one of the predominant characteristics of memory. We think in terms of images. Imagine an iPhone; have you imagined the device or the word? I already know the answer - the image of your favorite iPhone. Am I right?

1. Chain

The image chain method allows you to connect lists of facts and long concepts using associated images, so it is very useful to memorize information in order.

This technique is especially useful for VISGLO and VISANA.

Here's how you apply it:

- ✓ Associate a vivid image to each concept with a predominant color and a defined dimension.
- ✓ Dedicate the time necessary to visualize the details of the image to each association. For example, the word "house." Visualize how many floors and windows it has, the colors of the walls, etc. But don't miss too much because you can't spend more than ten seconds per image.
- ✓ Create the following image in your mind always using the same direction. If you have positioned the second image to the right of the previous house, continue like this.

Speaking of houses, you can follow the order of houses in your neighborhood or the footpath you take to college or work.

For this technique to work, you have to study even the smallest detail of the images during the visualization without creating great stories to associate with them, otherwise you will lose more time, distracting you from your goal. Remember, it is not about creating a plot for a Hollywood movie but quickly memorizing information.

2. The Russian Doll Method

Russian dolls are famous the world over. When you twist open the first doll, you find a smaller one inside, and so on, until you reach the last doll, the smallest.

This technique uses the same principle and aims to connect images to the concepts you want to memorize.

Instead of linking the images in a long chain, visualize them as if they were inside each other.

Visualize the image details as you did with the previous technique, then enlarge that image in your mind.

Zoom in until you see the next image inside it. Continue like this until you have viewed all images.

3. The Tree of Memory

In this case, the images are connected thanks to a reference image; the most classic is the tree.

Think of a tree you like and imagine every detail, such as what season it is, color and size.

Associate each branch with the images you want to memorize and imagine them as if you learned an image.

If the concepts you have to memorize are more complex, like having several levels of keywords for the same concept, you can use the structure of the branches to put the images in hierarchical order.

4. The Loci Technique

The last of the classic mnemonics I propose is 2,000 years old, but if applied correctly, it can be key to exams where you have to remember many concepts. I'm talking about the loci technique. This technique uses associative mnemonics to memorize long public speeches but also to embroider your developmental exams. Cicero in his time used it to remember hours-long public speeches without looking at notes.

The name derives from the Latin term locus and refers to the typology of associations used for memorization: the loci technique associates the arguments you want to remember with images of places you already know, such as your bedroom.

How does it work?

The next time you have to memorize a lengthy topic for a subject, do the following:

- ✓ Create a list of keywords and technical details you want to remember.
- ✓ Associate each keyword with an object in the room or place you have chosen, taking into account that it has to be a place you know well.
- ✓ Create fanciful associations between images to activate your emotional memory; you could relate your lamp to a bright theorem or the bed to a theme that makes you sleepy.

After you have made the associations, wander through your room whenever you have to review a chapter or when doing the exam or exhibition in class.

This technique will be particularly useful if your cognitive style is visual-analytical - VISANA. Above all, I advise you to use this technique when you draw a blank in the middle of the exam. When you learn to associate the key points of your exam with a place, you will not be left empty-minded because you will know where to search and retrieve the information.

Before I continue, I want to teach you how to use these techniques to study a 200-page book in two hours.

By applying some of the techniques seen so far, you can easily study a 200-page book in two hours.

1. Imagine you have to study a 200-page book. Each page contains 150 words, totalling 30,000 words.
2. Applying the fast-reading and organization techniques I have taught you can double your reading speed with 100% comprehension, so after 60 minutes, you will have finished the first reading.
3. The information you have read then goes inside a mind map, which with a little practice will take 25 minutes, with about 5 minutes to make the map of each chapter.
4. In each center of the map, you will associate an image with the topic you are on so you can distinguish them from each other. 5 minutes.
5. Finally, you will use the loci technique to memorize the maps. Choose a room in your house for each map, and associate each branch with an object in the room, for example, the first branch on the door. 15 minutes.
6. Then put the maps on the ground following the puzzle technique. Another 15 minutes.

And so you learn a 200-page book in just two hours. Now imagine it would take 10 times longer, so 20 hours across 4 or 5 days. What would your university life be like if it took 20 hours to memorize all this information? Now you understand how using these techniques consistently can determine your academic future.

Congratulations, you have saved yourself a lot of time and hassle with your study workload, giving you more time to do the things you love, and you have also arrived at the last module.

Chapter 8
Exposure

Wave Goodbye to Stage Fright

In this part, the memorization techniques learned in the previous chapter will be crucial. By having full control over the information, it is much easier to prepare for a presentation. The biggest challenge is overcoming nerves that can debilitate you and turn your thoughts to mush. Once confident in what you know, you can focus all your energy on how you're going to convey the information, not on remembering it.

Welcome to this last module, where we will talk about two main topics:

1. **Stress management**
2. **How to communicate 100% what we want**

Stress: enemy turned friend.

To know how to manage stress, you first have to know what kind of stress you are experiencing. There are stress periods caused by study:

- ✓ The first is the one you feel while studying. It's highly likely that you do not feel safe because you have experienced mishaps and mistakes, failed exams or scored lower than expected.
- ✓ Stress before the exam.
- ✓ Stress during the exam.

In general, stress is considered a response to a stressful stimulus. Today, however, as a result of the concept evolution, stress has been attributed to negative connotations that only harm our mind and body, usually because stress is associated with negative experiences and emotions that wear us down physically and mentally. This does not necessarily have to be the case, especially when stress is a mechanism we possess for our adaptability and survival.

According to World Health Organization, stress is usually identified as "preparation, defense and activation to face life situations more or less adequately."

This allows us to turn around the meaning related to the negative effects of stress and place the term more neutrally. According to the same authors, there are two main types of stress: productive or positive stress, associated with well-being facilitating responses such as the enabling of effective and powerful responses; and destructive stress, characterized by suffering negative tensions and poor efficacy in the body's response.

Stress will never disappear from our lives because it is part of our body's natural mechanisms to cope with situations of external or internal pressure. In a way, it is beneficial that we go through periods and processes of stress because sometimes these are the impulses we need to get out of adverse situations. The problem, obviously, arises when stress, instead of moving or pushing us towards a solution, leaves us disabled and frozen, making it difficult to make a conscious and rational decision, even if this means fleeing from the situation.

Stress manifests itself through mental and physical symptoms:

- ✓ Mental symptoms: consist of irritability, sleep problems, tiredness, sadness, worry, and difficulty concentrating.
- ✓ Physical symptoms: dry mouth, sweaty palms, muscle tension and back pain, breathing problems, dizziness, increased heart rate.

How to Cope When Stress Occurs

Change perspective: see stressful situations as opportunities to create and resolve and not as factors that threaten your integrity. This willing attitude to solve a problem redirects the energies that stress is consuming and transfers them to action.

- ✓ **Organization is key:** having an organized lifestyle and having foresight, so you know what's in store goes a long way. Time management and good administration are essential to give you greater control over what happens to you daily.
- ✓ **Sleep and unplug:** not allowing yourself to worry when in bed. It's important to let this space be immune to all internal and external influences and is solely and exclusively for rest.
- ✓ **Recognize what stresses you:** this awareness arises from analyzing your current and past states. We remember experiences and extract what we consider important to take action.

First, I'll talk about managing stress during the exam: from start to finish.

The second phase involves the night before and morning of the exam.

In the third phase, we will look at how to express your ideas and preparation so your emotions do not harm the result. I will give you techniques to apply. Some you will have to customize, others you won't.

Creative Visualization

Before the exam, you may feel unprepared. If so, there are two very important factors: one, you are afraid of the test because you think you won't know the answers, and two, you imagine a scenario where you fail. Your imagination is a powerful tool, and what you visualize changes your emotional state.

Our minds cannot recognize an image that has visualized a real event, for example, while sleeping, you have a nightmare about wolves following you through a forest and fear they will kill you. Your breath changes and your heart rate increases until, suddenly, you wake up! Your mind cannot perceive the difference between the dream and reality straightaway.

If you plan to visualize, ensure it is a creative visualization, imagining everything will turn out fine because by visualizing the assessed presentation in a specific way, you will be reviewing your content. Furthermore, because you imagine answering what you already know, your brain will be predisposed and will believe you already had that experience, so when the day comes, you are already on top, and your stress level declines. Program your brain to decrease your stress level.

It's important not to start visualizing when stressed, though. Only begin when you are studying, from day one, because your mind creates stress and must be programmed to manage it.

Sub Modality

Traumatic events also generate stress such as bad experiences at school that include failing an exam or losing your lecture notes. These raise stress levels.

If you do not change you perceive traumatic events, your stress level will also not change because you are still clinging to painful past events. The technique you can use here is called the cinema technique.

In this technique, you act like a film director. When you remember something, an image is created in your mind. Try to remember the last time you saw the sea, and your mind will conjure up an image which can have several characteristics:

It may or may not have color.

It can be a video or static image.

You can see yourself and others who see the image from another perspective. Or you can see from your eyes at the moment of recollection.

Each memory is associated with a good or bad feeling, which is associated with an emotion.

Every memory has characteristics, acting like a film director and directing your memory. Using the example of the sea, first it can be a static image and you can move it, add sound, enlarge or shrink it. Close your eyes and imagine that memory. If it is a video, add sound; if an image, change the color to black and white.

Now you know you can change your memories, imagine a white dog with yellow spots spewing fire. Our capacity for imagination is vast, so when you change the characteristics of the image, your emotion will also change.

If you feel uncomfortable about any memory related to the study, try changing it and the bad feeling connected to it. The wonderful thing about this technique is changing any emotion linked to a memory.

Managing stress before an exam is easy. It is difficult to do it when you are already in a bad state.

To help you in those moments, I have created the Bonus "Never stress again during a university exam."

The Hulk Technique

Hulk has a distinctive feature. Whenever he gets stressed or angry, he goes from normal to a giant green man with bulging muscles. Let's say, for argument's sake, this is your way of releasing stress.

This technique works similarly, and although you will not ruin any nice shirts in the process, you will get rid of tension and stress. When you are speaking in public or presenting for an exam, it is normal for your tension to increase, but it has to be released somewhere, and the way to vent is by tensing the muscles as if you were in the gym. Keep them tensed for as long as possible, and then relax. Complete some repetitions until all your adrenaline has toned your biceps and abdomen to some degree.

The Technique of the Four Elements

This technique is based on using breathing in four different ways using colors, depending on the situation you find yourself in.

Water

The water element technique is used when you need to calm yourself, such as when preparing for something important like an exam. You can use it to manage stress during your studies.

1. Inhale white light slowly through your nose.
2. Exhale slowly from the mouth, visualizing gray smoke escaping.

Earth

The earth element technique is used when you are scared, perhaps from past trauma, causing your heart to accelerate. It happens during exams when you encounter a question you do not know how to answer. Use this technique to avoid a blockage.

1. Inhale slowly through the nose.
2. Exhale quickly through the mouth.

Fire

The fire element technique is used when sensing danger when you need to calm down to be able to act but also have to remain alert. It is a technique you can use anytime before the exam when you need to be focused but calm.

1. Inhale quickly through the nose.
2. Exhale powerfully from the mouth, teeth and jaw clenched to help you release the tension.

Air

The air element technique is used when panicking and need to calm down.

1. Inhale quickly using your mouth this time.
2. Exhale quickly from your mouth.

It's similar to hyperventilating, except you can only do it ten times. No more, no less.

Your breath is your best ally in stress management, and now you know how to use it.

Leave Them With Their Mouths Open

Being relaxed makes it easier to speak in front of an audience, but it is not enough. Your poise and preparation also play an important role.

To improve your presentation, especially in terms of fluency and composure in delivery, I recommend you practice your speech out loud. Repeating your content out loud a couple of times not only helps you to remember but also gets your vocal muscles used to pronouncing difficult words, making your body interpret the speech with greater ease. In essence, this practice connects body and voice in harmony.

You can train the way you express yourself in three ways:

1. Predict what questions you will be asked, at least twenty.
2. Mentally repeat the speech.
3. 3. Using the creative visualization technique, imagine yourself in front of the teacher, and they ask you a question that you answer perfectly. Focus on how you deliver your answer, not what you'll say.

Good communication has to be consistent. Your body and voice must be aligned, leading us to the three levels of communication you can apply when practicing your delivery:

They are verbal, non-verbal and paraverbal language:

- ✓ Verbal communication is the vocabulary, what you say.
- ✓ Nonverbal communication is your body language, hand gestures, and movements you make.
- ✓ Paraverbal communication is the tone and rhythm of your voice when you speak.

Record yourself or practice in front of a mirror, moving around the space as remaining static on stage will only increase your stress level. Try to speak with a loud and confident voice, as this will give you confidence, and your words will flow with greater intensity.

You're calm, you're relaxed, your shirt hasn't burst open and your skin has not turned green. You're ready to pass any exam before you. Well, almost. You just need to read the next chapter, and you'll be raring to go!

Chapter 9
The Lord of Exams

Ready to learn how to pass any exam? Did you know exams also have tricks and rules? All right, let's get stuck in!

- ✓ General Tips: Whenever you can, prepare for classes in advance. Anticipating the study or reviewing the planned content, you will concentrate better and understand the topic more easily.
- ✓ Note the arguments the teacher explains with more emphasis, especially if they propose them as exam questions.
- ✓ Always ask for clarification if something is unclear. Your classmates will thank you, and the teacher will appreciate your interest and courage.
- ✓ Listen to what your classmates say about their exams and ask how they fared. Collect the maximum information.
- ✓ Study the corrected homework carefully and pay attention to your weak points in class.

Development Exams

This type of exam usually causes more anxiety in people who worry about exam preparation than in those afraid to speak in public. Two different types of stress lead to the same result: suspense. Here are some practical tips to pass the written tests.

Ask and Investigate

Always try to get more information beyond the date of the exam. Will there be special topics? Will they be open or closed questions? How many questions will there be? Will there also be exercises?

Organize Your Time

Read the questions, taking into account the time allocated for each question. Write a few lines for each answer instead of strengthening the one(s) you master. Be balanced in your time management so you finish with nothing lacking.

Don't Waste Time on Exercises You Don't Know

If you become stumped, move on to the next question and return later when you have answered everything else. Whatever you do, do not skip all the questions because you don't know the answer 100%. If you did this, you risk reaching the end without having finished anything.

Read Questions Carefully Several Times

Even those you don't know how to answer. If you study the question carefully, you may find some ideas to answer them. On the other hand, seemingly easy questions sometimes hide a trap, so take your time and read carefully, as it is time well spent.

Set Aside Time for a Final Review

Leave a little time at the end to re-read everything. It's likely you will pick up errors and need to make adjustments. Also, pay attention to syntax, grammar, lexicon, and logic. You don't want to lose points for careless mistakes.

Being Tidy Counts

Try to be tidy. I know that exam nerves may affect your writing and that neatness is the least of your concerns, but put yourself in the teacher's shoes when it comes to marking. A messy answer could cost you points.

Follow the Directions

Respect the directions in the questions. If it says write a maximum of 200 words, it is a waste of time to write more, even if you have more to say, because the teacher will not give you extra marks. In fact, you may even be penalized for writing over the word count.

Cutlets

I cannot emphasize the importance of keywords enough. The famous chops are keywords chosen to develop the theme. In the chop, you put a word that allows you to remember the concept. The goal is to convince the examiner of your preparation, not that you have memorized the content without any understanding, so use the keywords and develop the rest of the answer with your own words., You should earn many points because the teacher will see the keywords and realize you have understood the topic question.

Multiple Choice Exams

Let's talk about the different types of exams. There are, in fact, ways to pass the exam without having studied much. First, answer questions you already know without wasting time on those you don't.

Then take care of the ones you have left blank, following a series of rules to help you earn several more points. Remember that, as a general rule, never leave an answer blank, and ensure you follow these rules:

Intuition Deceives

Regarding multiple choice exams, they are designed by people whose objective is to deceive and confuse you to identify who is prepared and who is not. The truth is that there are ways to detect the psychology behind the exam, and the trick is never to go by intuition. If there is a question that has new word answers and you think that might be the answer, don't trust your intuition.

You should keep in mind that the deposit memory is perfect. This means the memory can recognize the words it already knows. All the information that has been stored inside the memory has been stored and your brain is able to recognize what it has already seen, so if you see an answer with words you do not recognize, it will not be the correct one.

Similar Meanings

Imagine, for example, you have found an answer that is similar to another, obviously you have to take into account that whoever created the exam wants to know your knowledge of the subject, so where there are similar meanings but not the same, it is often the right answer. Focus on those two options.

Nothing is Absolute

With the exception of mathematics, very few things are absolute in the exam world. When you come across this type of answer, discard it, it is not the correct option.

Far from Extremes

I recommend avoiding extreme answers. For example, imagine you have four possible answers in a mathematics exam. A = 1487, B = 26, C = 36 and D = -182. Eliminate the first option because it is much larger than the others. Also, eliminate the last option because it is a negative number. Therefore, the correct answer is either B or C.

The Joker

It is interesting when we have a question with four options, one being the dreaded "all the above" or one with several correct answers. If there is more than one, that is likely the right answer.

Repeat

Sometimes repetition helps. Imagine a question with four possible answers. A has as option xx, kk, B has zzz, xx, C has xx, tt, and D has zzz, xx. You see some answers contain repeated vocabulary. Using logic and a little calculation, you can determine the correct answer. Let's imagine you have no clue about the answer but see the value x has been repeated. Eliminate the answer that does not repeat the vocabulary and see which ones resemble each other.

The Answer to the Question

The answer may be within the question but you have not noticed, so ensure you read the statement carefully.

Opposites

Opposites attract! Imagine you have a question and three answers: A, increases, B, decreases or C, stays the same. In most instances, focus on the opposites because one is often the correct answer.

Extraordinary Results

You must take into account the study method, that everything I have taught you is true. It will help you get a better score, but you must know how to face an exam. To be successful with the method, you must also have a good attitude, know how to read, remember what you have read and studied, and, above all, be prepared so when you arrive at an exam, you know what to do.

Science and Humanism

Let's see what happens when applying the nine tips you have seen by eliminating at least one of the multiple answers related to the questions that would otherwise be left blank.

I return to the above examples:

Example 1:

- ✓ There are 10 questions that we cannot answer.
- ✓ There are 5 options for each question, and we have not been able to rule out any.
- ✓ Each correct answer is awarded 1 point.
- ✓ For each incorrect answer, -0.5 points is awarded.
- ✓ Blank boxes do not alter the score.

This is the most complicated scenario since the margin for error is minimal. We can reason and seek the wrong answers, but as you will see, rarely is it convenient to answer.

We can try our luck if we have any doubts about the 3 probabilities, though in this case, the statistical calculation does not help because the result would be the same as if you had left the box blank. On the other hand, if you can eliminate 3 of the 5 possible answers, you are left with two possibilities, and the following will happen:

For each question, we have a 50-50 chance of getting it right (1/2 = 0.5) and, therefore, a 50-50 chance of getting it wrong (1/2 = 0.5). The approaches to which we do not know how to answer are 10 so:

Score per correct answer (out of 10): 0.5 x 10 x (+1) = +5

Where: 0.5 is the probability (calculated before) of getting the answer right, 10 being the number of questions to which we do not know how to answer, and the score attributed to a correct question is (+1).

Score for incorrect answer (out of 10): 0.5 x 10 x (- 0.5) = - 2.5
Where: 0.5 is the possibility (calculated before) of making mistakes, 10 is the number of questions we do not know how to answer, and the score applied to an incorrect answer is (-0.5).

Total points if we decide to answer: + 5 – 2.5 = + 2. 5
Total points if we decide not to answer: 10 x 0 = 0

Conclusion: You get 2.5 additional points for every ten questions you do not know the answer, but where you eliminate three answers that you consider absurd.

Example 2:

- ✓ There are 10 questions we cannot answer.
- ✓ There are 5 options for each question and we have not been able to rule out any.
- ✓ Each correct answer is awarded 1 point.
- ✓ Each incorrect answer is awarded -0.25 points.
- ✓ Blank boxes do not alter the score.

In this case, the speech is more interesting because the impact of an error on the final score is greatly reduced. Here it is convenient to label answers as absurd and look for the right answers, as you will see it is convenient to answer in practically all cases. In addition, we can decide whether to attempt luck when we have not managed to eliminate any of the 5 possibilities, as the final result does not vary if we simply leave the boxes blank, shown in the statistics. On the other hand, it is advisable to always answer when, by elimination, we have managed to discard at least 1 of the 5 possible answers.

In this case, the choice is reduced to 4, 3 or 2 alternatives (clearly the more discards, the better) and the following happens:

For each question, we have a 1 in 4 chance of getting it right (1/4 = 0.25) and therefore 3 in 4 chance of getting it wrong (3/4 = 0.75). The approaches to which we do not know how to answer are 10, so:

Score per correct answer (out of 10): 0.25 x 10 x (+1) = +2.5 where: 0.25 is the probability (calculated before) of getting the correct answer right, 10 being the number of questions we do not know how to answer, the score attributed to a correct question is (+1).

Score for incorrect answer (out of 10): 0.75 x 10 x (-0.25) = – 1.875 Where: 0.75 is the possibility (calculated before) of making a mistake, 10 is the number of questions we do not know how to answer, the score applied to an incorrect answer is (-0.25).

Total points if we decide to answer: + 2.5 – 1.875 = 0.625
Total points if we decide not to answer: 10 x 0 = 0

Conclusion: You receive 0.625 points for every 10 questions you do not answer, but manage to eliminate at least one of the options that seem absurd to you and answer those that remain. If you discard 2 possible answers (there is a 1 in 3 chance to guess correctly), it is an extra 1.65 points. If you eliminate 3 (1 in 2 chance of getting it right), it is an additional 3.75 points. They are points you would not have obtained, leaving the boxes blank.

Example 3:

- ✓ There are 10 questions we cannot answer.
- ✓ There are 5 options for each question, and we have not been able to rule out any.
- ✓ Each correct answer is awarded 1 point.
- ✓ For each incorrect answer, -0.33 points are awarded.
- ✓ Blank boxes do not alter the score.

In this case, as in the previous one, it is more convenient to answer. We can start by trying our luck when we have not eliminated any of the 5 possibilities because, as we have seen before, the final result varies positively. It is worth answering whether we have been able to rule out at least 1 of the 4 possible answers. In this case, the choice is reduced to 2 or 3 options (of course, the more options we eliminate, the better), and the following happens:

For each question, we have a 1-3 chance to get it right (1/3 = 0.33) and, therefore, 2 out of 3 chances to get it wrong (2/3 = 0.66). The approaches to which we do not know how to answer are 10, so:

Score per correct answer (out of 10): 0.33 x 10 x (+1) = + 3.3 where: 0.33 is the probability (calculated before) of getting the correct answer right, 10 being the number of questions we do not know how to answer, the score attributed to a correct question is (+1).

Score for incorrect answer (out of 10): 0.66 x 10 x (- 0.33) = - 2.178 where: 0.66 is the possibility (calculated before) of making mistakes, 10 is the number of questions we do not know how to answer, and the score applied to an incorrect answer is (-0.33).

Total points if we decide to answer: + 3.3 – 2.178 = + 1.122

Total points if we decide not to answer: 10 x 0 = 0

Conclusion: If you eliminate at least 1 of the options that seem absurd to you and mark 1 of the rest, you get 1.122 points for every ten questions you do not know the answer.

If you eliminate 2 answer options, you have a chance between 2 of getting it right, which is an additional 3.35 points. These are points you would not have achieved if you had not answered.

Example 4:

- ✓ There are 10 questions that we cannot answer.
- ✓ There are 5 options for each question, and we have not been able to rule out any.
- ✓ Each correct answer is awarded 1 point.
- ✓ Each incorrect answer is awarded -0.3 points.
- ✓ Each blank box is awarded 0.1 points.

In this case, it is also advisable to always answer. We can attempt luck because if we have not managed to eliminate any of the 5 options, it is convenient to answer even more if we have eliminated at least 1 of the 5 possible options. In this case, the choice is limited to 2, 3 or 4 options (of course, the more that are eliminated, the better) and the following happens:

For each question, we have a 1 in 4 chance of getting it right (1/4 = 0.25) and, therefore, 3 in 4 chances of getting it wrong (3/4 = 0.75). The approaches to which we do not know how to answer are 10, so:

Score per correct answer (out of 10): 0.25 x 10 x (+1) = + 2.5 where: 0.33 is the probability (calculated before) of getting the correct answer right, 10 is the number of questions we do not know how to answer, and the score attributed to a correct question is (+1).

Score for incorrect answer (out of 10): 0.75 x 10 x (- 0.33) = -2.25 where: 0.75 is the possibility (calculated before) of making mistakes, 10 is the number of questions we do not know how to answer and the score applied to an incorrect answer is (-0.3).

Total points if we decide to answer: + 2.5 – 2.25 = 0.25
Total points if we decide not to answer: 10 x (-0.1) = -1

Conclusion: You receive 1.25 points more for every ten questions you do not know how to answer and that if you had left blank, would constitute a penalty of -1 point, so you can eliminate at least 1 of the answers and answer those that remain. If you eliminate 2 (1 in 3 chances to get it right), that's an additional 2.32 points. If you manage to eliminate up to 3, achieving 1 instead of 2 is 4.5 points more.

Now you know some more stratagem to accompany luck, your chances of guessing the right answer increases considerably., Still, trying to pass an exam can be like playing roulette in the casino as a part of you feels the fear of an uncertain outcome. In this case, it is not a sensation but a reality. Therefore, before taking a high-stakes exam, use these new strategies to simulate the exam, but, above all, STUDY. Download past exams from the Internet and proceed as if it were the real exam. Answer as best you can, leaving questions you don't know blank, and calculate your final score. Then go back to the unanswered questions and apply the strategies above.

Don't try only once, as statistics work best when you have lots of comparable data. In this way, you will realize which strategy works best for you.

One last thing. If you think applying statistical techniques is solely enough to pass a difficult exam, we sincerely apologize for leading you down the wrong path. These techniques work for prepared students and have shown due diligence throughout the exam revision process.

The best trick to pass a multiple-choice exam, or any exam for that matter, comes down to one important element: always be prepared!

Chapter 10
Your Style, Your Method

Now you know all the techniques, it's time to set up your own method. I have divided the best strategies according to your style and communication channel so you can use this book as if it were a custom-made suit.

The **A for Approach** is the same whether Global or Analytical, Visual or Verbal. It is a phase you cannot skip since it is the preamble to get the most out of your study.

To create your **Temple of Study**, choose the study cycle that best suits you and build your Master Plan to utilize your time.

The Study Method for a VISGLO

Visual-Global students need an overview when they begin their study and memorize information through images.

The best techniques for you are:

Reading

- ✓ Preview
- ✓ List of Distractions
- ✓ The Tangerine Technique
- ✓ Pointer

Comprehension

- ✓ Trailer Technique
- ✓ Youtube Technique
- ✓ Brainstorming
- ✓ Compass Technique

Organization

- ✓ **Keywords:** you do not require too many keywords or technical details; one or two keywords per concept will suffice. Of course, you have to fully understand what you are studying and do the verification.
- ✓ **Mind Maps:** To create your mind map, start by dividing the sheet into four quadrants and deciding the main branches to put in each quadrant. Before writing, think about how you will organize the information, and always start by writing all the main branches first so you have a global vision of the map. For details and child branches, use drawings instead of words whenever possible and use a different color for the main branch that represents a theme. This ensures your eyes perceive the information that is different from the one related in a single glance.
- ✓ **Notes in Class:** Before class, preview the chapter so you have a global vision of what the teacher will say and create the main branches of the map. During class, all you have to do is add the secondary ones.

Memory

- ✓ The Puzzle Technique
- ✓ Flashcards
- ✓ Image Method

The Study Method for a VISANA

Visual-Analytical need to deepen the information they are studying and memorize using very sharp images full of details.

Reading

- ✓ Preview: Go inside the chapter and read all the titles, subtitles, bold words, and everything that catches your eye.
- ✓ List of Distractions
- ✓ Technique of the Mandarin
- ✓ Pointer
- ✓ Understanding
- ✓ Short Film Technique
- ✓ Compass Technique
- ✓ Image Streaming

Organization

- ✓ **Keywords:** At first, while everything will seem important to you, before selecting the information, start asking yourself, "How can I summarize this concept with a couple of keywords?" If you need four instead of two, you can take them. As for the details, you can select all the ones that are necessary to complement the chosen keywords. In this phase, you can take any extras you want, just in case, although I recommend that whenever you take a word, you question whether it is essential. You must do the verification! You will realize some repeated or left-over words, as with the details.

Simply delete any repetitions and do not add them to the map.

✓ **Mind Maps:** Divide the sheet into four quadrants. With clear words and details, you can start creating the map with the first branch and continue adding the secondary and tertiary branches. Try to limit yourself to no more than four rings - main ring, secondary ring, and, at most, two more to add details. Otherwise you risk creating a giant branch full of unnecessary words. The branches have to reach the four divisions you have made to manage the space and avoid going overboard with the details. For details and child branches, use drawings instead of words whenever possible and use a different color for the main branch that represents a theme so your eyes perceive the information that is different from the related one in a single glance.

✓ **Class Notes:** Before class, use the short film technique so the points the teacher will deal with are clear in your mind and you have understood more about what see during class. In class, following the structure of clock hands, divide the sheet and start pointing at everything the teacher says that seems important to what you saw with the short film technique. I recommend you have two sheets, especially at the beginning, where you create the map in one and write down everything you do not know where to allocate on your map but seems important on the other. For example, a definition. Do not worry about messy handwriting. The important thing is you leave class with all the important information. Then, at home, create a clean map using the two sheets, and add all the details and extra information.

Memory

- ✓ Theatrical Representation
- ✓ Flashcards
- ✓ Image Method
- ✓ Loci Technique
- ✓ Stories and Tales

The Study Method for a VERANA

Before fully understanding the concept, **Verbal-Analytical** people have to familiarize themselves with the details. They need to write what they study to memorize and internalize the information.

Reading

- ✓ Preview: Enter the chapter and read all the titles, subtitles, words in bold, and everything that catches your attention.
- ✓ List of Distractions
- ✓ Tangerine Technique
- ✓ Pointer

Comprehension

- ✓ Short Film Technique
- ✓ Compass Technique
- ✓ Image Streaming

Organization

- ✓ Keywords: While everything will initially seem important to you, before selecting the information, start asking yourself, "How can I summarize this concept with a couple of keywords?" If you need four instead of two, you can take them. As for the details, you can select all the ones that are necessary to complement the chosen keywords. In this phase, you can take any extras you want, just in case, although I recommend that whenever you take a word, you question whether it is really important. You must do the **verification!** You will realize some repeated or left-over words, as with the details. Simply delete any repetitions and do not add them to the map.

✓ **Mind Maps:** Divide the sheet into four quadrants. With clear words and details, you can start creating the map with the first branch and continue adding the secondary and tertiary branches. Try to limit yourself to no more than four rings - main ring, secondary ring, and, at most, two more to add details. Otherwise you risk creating a giant branch full of unnecessary words. The branches have to reach the four divisions you have made to manage the space and avoid going overboard with the details. You can also use colors and drawings, especially if they remind you of sounds, but I recommend always writing the words and details in capital letters.

✓ **Class Notes:** Before class, use the short film technique so the points the teacher will deal with are clear in your mind and you have understood more about what see during class. In class, following the structure of clock hands, divide the sheet and start pointing at everything the teacher says that seems important to what you saw with the short film technique. I recommend you have two sheets, especially at the beginning, where you create the map in one and write down everything you do not know where to allocate on your map but seems important on the other. For example, a definition. Do not worry about messy handwriting. The important thing is you leave class with all the important information. Then, at home, create a clean map using the two sheets, and add all the details and extra information.

Memory

- ✓ Stories and Tales
- ✓ Audiobooks

The Study Method for a GLOVER

A **Global-Verbal** student needs a global vision of the arguments they study and uses written language to memorize.

Reading

- ✓ Preview
- ✓ List of Distractions
- ✓ The Mandarin Technique
- ✓ Pointer

Comprehension

- ✓ Trailer Technique
- ✓ Youtube Technique
- ✓ Brainstorming
- ✓ Compass Technique

Organization

- ✓ **Keywords:** you do not require too many keywords or technical details; one or two keywords per concept will suffice. Of course, you have to fully understand what you are studying and do the verification.
- ✓ **Mind Maps:** To create your mind map, start by dividing the sheet into four quadrants and deciding the main branches to put in each quadrant. Before writing, think about how you will organize the information, and always start by writing all the main branches first, so you have a global vision of the map. For details and child branches, use drawings instead of

words whenever possible and use a different color for the main branch representing a theme. This ensures your eyes perceive the information that is different from the one related in a single glance.

✓ **Notes in Class:** Before class, preview the chapter so you have a global vision of what the teacher will say and create the main branches of the map. During class, all you have to do is add the secondary ones.

Retention

✓ Puzzle Technique
✓ Repeat to your Grandpa
✓ Audiobooks

You have reached the end of the book. You have come a long way, acquiring a range of new techniques with a personalized study method you've been building since the start. By now, you should feel confident and ready to tackle any subject, any textbook in any academic situation. You should start to see improvements in your results if you employ the techniques and methods you have learned. You should also be proud of yourself.

We are at the end, but I'm not done yet. You don't think these techniques and methods only apply during your academic studies, do you? Think again. I have more in store for you because learning is a lifelong journey, and the real challenge awaits – your chosen career!

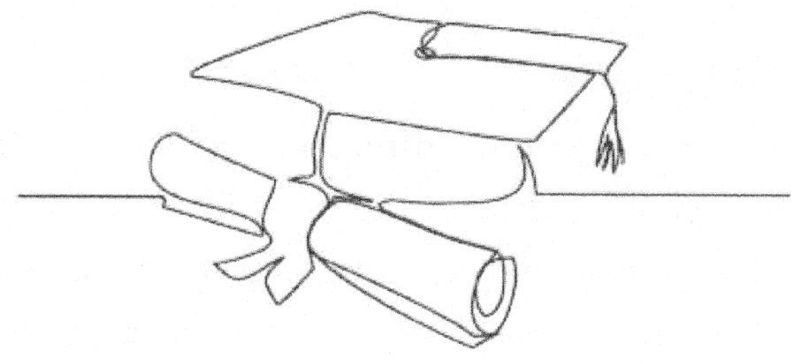

Chapter 11
Bonus: Your Dream Job

Unlike a college or university course, studying is a lifelong journey. The moment you stop learning is the moment you stop being receptive to new information, differences of opinion, and the willingness to challenge yourself.

You probably have an idea of what you would like to do when you finish your studies, whether it's the company you want to work for, the senior position you aspire to reach, or a vocation you wish to realize. In short, you have a dream to aspire to.

In the event you are still a little unclear about your future direction, either because you are just starting your career or because you have many areas in which you could specialize, I recommend you do some research. Take advantage of any downtime and browse the different specialties and job opportunities or additional study options to help you discern your goals. Having a clear direction after college or university is the first step to moving forward and realizing your dreams.

As Seneca said, a man without objectives is like a ship without a rudder - he drifts.

Without direction or purpose, drifting through your studies will end with a degree in your hand but without any idea what to do with it. This is one of the reasons why so many students end up working in an industry they have not studied for, which is a waste of time and money.

If you fit the profile of a drifter in its most respectful sense, I have homework to help you clarify.

Take advantage of social media to see what the people you admire are doing: where they work and what they've done to get there. You can browse the profiles of the companies or associations you like, watch their videos or search on Google.

If, on the other hand, you already have a clear direction, let's start.

Create the Professional You Want to Be

You must be looking forward to that moment where, finally, after so much study and academic pressure, you are ready to put everything into practice in the workplace of your dreams.

But to get there, you first have to stand out when applying for roles in your chosen career. You will be up against candidates who have more experience than you, so you will need to impress because a university degree and an attractive-looking CV are simply not enough. After all, you have slaved through four years of study but what do you really know about your industry other than industry terminology and anything your textbooks informed you about.

I do not want to detract from the title and all the effort you have made to obtain your qualification, but let's be realistic and call a spade a spade, those four years of study serve to prepare you for the beginning of a long career ahead with so much more to learn, so your first challenge is preparing a CV that enhances your character and achievements with little experience to go by. However, when you finish your degree, you have a series of experiences, skills and additional training.

Regarding what skills to include, this requires research to find out what a person does in the position you are applying for and the company's objective, core values, and mission so you can align your skills accordingly.

Also, find out what work experience the company desires, how many languages, what interpersonal skills, and what software programs you need to know or master.

Many graduates spend another two years doing internships, part-time jobs, additional courses, and learning languages before starting their careers, delaying the fulfillment of their career dreams.

If, on the other hand, you graduate prepared and knowledgeable of the industry you are ready to begin and the professional you want to be, you will be able to face any challenge.

That said, let's talk about how to create the perfect CV.

A Tailored CV

Remember I told you we are all different? That we all have different learning styles? Well, it's the same for companies.

Writing a template CV and sending it to every company does not work. It's lazy and does not always align with what companies seek.

You need a CV that stands out and sets you apart from all the others flooding company inboxes. Start by changing the format. The classic Word document with the photo in the top right corner has been relegated to history. If you want to distinguish yourself, start by creating a CV that captures your attention at a glance.

You do not need a master's degree in graphic design as online platforms such as Canva offer hundreds of artistic ready-made templates.

Visual delight is one thing, content is quite another. After capturing the company's attention, they will want to see what makes you the right fit for their organization and how your values and goals match theirs. This is why a CV must be tailored.

Every job position and company has different characteristics, so you have to find out what they are and link them to your profile and experience recorded in your CV. It should be the first thing they see, making you stand out as the ideal candidate for an interview.

Again, research is essential in this phase since it will allow you to be one step ahead of your competition and demonstrate your preparation, enthusiasm, and professionalism.

Now you are ready!

Using this book as your guide, dedicate some time to it and learn to study well. Remember that practice makes perfect, and if you want to achieve great results, you have to start with a positive attitude and the desire to do well.

Now you know how the method works, you can re-read the book from the beginning and apply those techniques that, based on your cognitive style, best suit you. You may find it difficult to break from the tradition of reading and repeating or believe doing it this new way means dedicating more time. But, like learning to ride a bike, it took time and a few nasty falls on the concrete to reach a level where it became second nature. You just need to persevere. Learning how to study better is not like riding a bicycle but driving a Ferrari because when you press the accelerator, you reach your destination much faster. It is up to you to learn to master the skills and techniques and dare to go all the way to discover what you can achieve if you apply what you have learned in this book.

More than 50,000 university students worldwide have done it, now it's your turn!

I wish you great results, stress-free academic study providing you with the work-life balance we all deserve, a prosperous career where you achieve your lifelong goals and the life you dream of.

Become the Successful Professional You're Meant to Be

As I stated at the beginning of this book, I firmly believe we never stop learning even after school. In business, there is so much to learn every day if you really want to impact the world with your business. I believe learning facilitates that impact because the more you learn, the more you know, and the more knowledgeable you are, the more confidence you have to shape what you want to create.

The moment you stop learning, you stop growing. In nature, the only things that don't grow are dead. People stop learning not because they choose to but because they have had learning blocks since their school days. No one has taught them an alternative method, so they simply give up.

The business process is a creative one. If you're an entrepreneur, there are times when you feel invincible and unshakeable and other times when you feel stuck and at a loss. This bonus chapter will help you clarify the professional you want to be.

There are three last things I want to give you today. We talked about mindset, and I believe a professional with all the right strategies but a poor mindset will inevitably fail in their endeavors. Techniques are pointless without heart. Our heart provides the spark and the willingness to keep growing and never stop learning. Sometimes we forget about it, and that's when we lose our vision, light, and sense of creation. Have you ever felt like a hamster running endlessly in a wheel? What do you do at that moment?

Why does this happen?

Before modern civilization, humankind was exposed to numerous threats, including wild animals such as tigers and bears. Every day was a fight for survival in inhospitable environments. So every morning, they woke up believing the worst would happen to them to prevent it from coming true, to survive. They needed to learn to think about either fighting, running, or hiding." Our brains had to engage in survival mode, the difference between life or death. As a result, we programmed our brain to think negatively to achieve a positive outcome, in this case, survival. Unless you are at the mountain peaks in Colorado, we don't have to concern ourselves about an imminent bear attack. But our brains still focus on negative things, so we have to interrupt this pattern and learn how to go from negative emotions to elevated emotions. Our emotions greatly influence our results, as you learned at the beginning of this book. What we feel, we create. So, how do we change our focus?

In the Trailer technique, when you ask your brain different questions, your brain will give you different answers. Therefore, each question has an answer. Our brains crave these answers. It's like when someone asks you in the car: "Who sings this song?" Perhaps you don't know straight away, but it bugs you while you wrack your brains for the answer. Then, while you're washing your dishes two days later, it pops into your brain out of nowhere: "Whitney Houston!" You thought you had stopped thinking about it, but your brain needed to find the answer.

So, in short, negative thinking leads to negative outcomes and a poor emotional state.

The Spark Technique

We need to reactivate the spark in our hearts. It's a combination of two techniques you already know and one more.

- ✓ Hulk Technique to release your tension
- ✓ Earth Breathing Technique
- ✓ Start jumping for one minute to music you love and smile while you're doing it! You may feel silly initially, which is why it works so well. You're creating a disconnection between what your brain expects from your negative state of frustration or anxiety and your actions. It doesn't recognize what's happening at the moment, but you're coming out of an emotional state you don't like.
- ✓ When the music finishes and your breath catches again, stop and place your hand over your heart and feel it beating. You are alive!

Now ask yourself different questions:

- ✓ What am I grateful for?
- ✓ Who do I love in my life?
- ✓ What do I love about my life?
- ✓ To whom am I grateful in my life?

Now your brain is thinking about those precious things, and you are transitioning to a better emotional state that will allow you to find a real solution to what's happening in your business. Or establish a better connection to what you want to achieve.

Remember the heart is the first thing your mother saw in her womb. It's the first thing we develop before our brain. There's an important message: use your heart to give life to your business, project and, dreams.

Repeat this process anytime you feel emotions you want to change. The more you do it, the more your brain will create a more desirable connection with new questions and answers that empower you.

A Super Producer

Among all the things you may need to learn for your business, there are also many other tasks you have to address. But it comes at a cost. It's so easy to become swamped and stressed as everything is always important and urgent, making us super busy, and yet we may find we are not nearly as productive as we need to be. Here is one of the many techniques I can teach you to manage productivity satisfaction.

Prioritize

Prioritize is a great buzz word but when under stress, everything seems like a priority. What I recommend is:

- ✓ Take your TO-DO list and number your items from 1 to 10.
- ✓ Number 1 is the highest priority, 10 is the lowest.
- ✓ Scientifically speaking, our brain feels satisfied if we fulfill at least the first three daily priorities. But what if you don't have time?

To-do List Block

- ✓ In your calendar, always schedule a block of time when you can recover from the tasks piling up during the day to fulfil the first three priorities.

By completing the first three priorities based on your goal that day, you're going to feel satisfied.

Your achievements today will make you feel more satisfied tomorrow, even if there are other items you didn't cross off. Also, you will have more energy, and guess what? You're likely to execute

the other items on your to-do list during your recovery period, creating a virtuous cycle of satisfaction that will generate more motivation, focus and productivity!

Look out for my next book as you will discover how to achieve unlimited productivity based on your cognitive styles.

Not everyone organizes information the same way as explored in the cognitive styles chapter. I cannot wait to share more with you.

Study Cases

In the following study cases, you'll be introduced to people just like you who took time out of their busy lives to learn and achieve new results. Sometimes, it's stories of others who inspire us with new ideas. The experiences of others can create new connections and points of view, breathing life into your mind, and with your actions, those ideas take form in reality. That's why I include these experiences with you to give your brain a new, enriching vision, but most of all, a great opportunity to decide a new direction or positive changes, improving your path to bring you new results that seem unfathomable.

Pay attention to how simple they made it.

Renatus Company – How to be financially free by unblocking your learning blocks.

Renatus is community-focused, ensuring it makes a positive impact on the world. The wealth generated through business ownership and real estate investments allows individuals to change America's economic landscape, empowering one million entrepreneurs with this wealth creation system.

One of the fastest-growing companies for the past three years, Renatus has received statewide attention by winning the Best of State award for the past five years, including three different categories: Seminar Education, Educational Literature, and Trade Publication.

In a recent poll of 187 students, 4852 real estate deals were completed after purchasing the Renatus education. That's an average of 25.9 transactions per person, highlighting how effective the education truly is.

Many people may be attracted to real estate or think they are not interested because they don't know how good real estate can be with the right knowledge.

Yes, real estate can be hard without the know-how. Bob Snyder, founder of Renatus, runs the number-one educational service for real estate investors and entrepreneurs in the country. Their online video library contains more than 400 hours of training, assessments, note-taking capabilities and task creation. I thought great, but…

What if you're studying but can't recall the knowledge you learned?

Here is a simple equation:

Perfect method = Study = Retain/learn = Knowledge = Feel confident = Application = Results = Achieve my goal.

If you have a perfect method to study, you retain and learn. This creates knowledge, which makes you feel confident, so now you feel good about applying the things you know because you can recall them, achieve your results and move forward.

This education goes precisely to the point of taking actions to achieve your financial freedom through real estate and leveraging your current business. I applied it. All courses are taught by "practitioner instructors" who work hands-on in the areas they teach, so customers can be confident that these strategies apply to real life.

You have no idea how many people get stuck in their path because they have learning blocks, and they don't know. How can you apply things you can't recall or retain? How could you feel confident to apply the things you can't remember at that moment? How can you say "yes" to a deal when inside, you lack the knowledge to move forward?

Sometimes, what you're studying, the material you're studying is not the problem. Sure, it's not the problem of this education since I studied and applied it :)

Almost always, if everyone is achieving results based on the their knowledge except you, it's a problem with the method that makes you inadequate to applying the things you're learning, leaving you feeling stuck.

After people took the Genius course, they could apply these study methods and learn how to reduce taxes thanks to tax strategies, for example, feeling good enough to talk to the air accountant and tell them strategies they didn't even know existed, and many, including me, saved thousands of dollars in taxes. The number of students who felt capable of studying better after adopting their ideal method is countless.

Tom – from feeling overwhelmed to a multimillion-dollar deal.

"I love how much education Renatus offers, but 400 hours of information is a lot! Before the Genius course, I wanted to try all the different strategies, but it was overwhelming! I would get mired in details while analyzing deals, afraid I was missing something or forgetting something important. It was stressful, and I hate to think of how many deals I missed out on because I was paralyzed by anxiety. After doing the Genius course, I know I will recall everything I need when I need it. This has freed up so much time and given me the confidence to triple my short-term rental business! Not only have I done more deals in the last few months than in the last few years, but I am doing a new multimillion-dollar commercial build that I wouldn't even have had the courage to analyze before I met Cosimo!"

Thanks to Renatus, I have access to the investing knowledge I need. Thanks to the Genius course, I can access that knowledge when I need it!

Michael Huggins – either busy or productive.

"I work from home as a real estate investor and as I've taken on more projects and gotten busier, I needed to find a way to stay out of overwhelm and stay organized. I also have two kids under two. Being busy combined with a weak style of note-taking was costing me too much opportunity. After meeting Cosimo and taking the Genius course I feel a lot more confident, and I am more productive about the bigger projects such as commercial real estate development, Eco-Tourism and parenting; I'm taking on and organizing my time to make sure I'm still there for my family. I am utilizing techniques like speed reading and mind maps, which have made it easier for me to hit my goals. I'm very grateful that our paths have crossed!"

Damon M. Greene – how to organize yourself to create at least 1000 leads in a day.

When I met Damon, he wasn't only an extraordinary coach in his industry, but he was so swamped with clients that it was taking a long time to launch his online program. He was creating content and putting together programmers for a website, landing pages and everything else to guarantee product and satisfaction. He wanted to do a workshop and teach to bigger audiences as soon as possible, but his learning block in organization hindered him from finding extra time to complete his project. Unfortunately, our brains would love to do many things, but it shuts down your dreams if it doesn't retrieve resources to accomplish the task or topic at hand, leaving you at a loss. No method = slow progress.

If you had unlimited time and energy, what would you do?

Here is Damon's story.

"After going through and understanding this course, I have been able to organize my business and fast-track results without being overwhelmed and flying by the seat of my pants like I was. Thanks to these strategic and learning techniques, I had been doing monthly workshops that added an extra 10K to my monthly sales just by being more organized with reading, consuming information faster, and retaining it. Mind Map was a tool I thought I knew, but the way they explained and customized it for me was mind-blowing. I haven't started yet on my language learning and memorization, but I'm really excited to be able to speak more fluently and communicate in Spanish by the end of 2022."

What's thirty days from now? Please count.

Now imagine I tell you you'll launch your program and live your dream on that day? How would you feel? Nothing happens unless first you dream and then believe in it. You can achieve this with the right method, I promise.

Gabriela – passing the Bar Exam stress-free.

If you're taking the Bar Exam to become a lawyer, this story will help you.

Gabriela Picazo-Batista and I just got out of court, and so I wanted to take a moment to tell you about my experience with the Genius course. I heard about it through my previous boss when I was a law student who was an attorney. He had taken the course and had recommended it to me because he knew I was about to graduate.

"I was beginning my bar prep for the Bar Exam, and he thought it would be beneficial to take the course to help me with my studying. To give you an idea of what the Bar Exam entails and what the studying process looks like, we had to remember an entire semester's worth of classes in one day! So we had to learn all the rules for criminal law in Georgia in one day! Plus everything you did during your years in college. And so, when I saw I was extremely overwhelmed and thought to myself: "How am I going to do this? How do people do this?" I spoke to Cosimo, and I let him know what my concerns were and what my goals were in taking the course! He made me feel at ease, so I ended up taking that chance and took the course in the middle of my bar prep, and I have absolutely zero regrets! Not only was I able to take the course with amazing people, but I also got individualized mentorship where Cosimo helped me with specific learning blocks that I was experiencing and needed to know to help me overcome them. For example, my anxiety and stress, how to do mind mapping. He helped me with speed-reading techniques, practical steps to really help me specifically for studying, and I really felt my trust in him and myself!

I used the techniques throughout my studying and when I took the Bar Exam, I didn't feel as nervous as I thought I would because I felt very prepared. I was READY, and after that I had to wait ten weeks, probably the most nerve-wracking part of the process, having to wait for those results for ten weeks, Later, I found out my results, and one of the first things I did was text both my mom and Cosimo to let them know I had passed. It was a very happy moment for me and my family, and I owe a lot of that to Cosimo and the Genius course. I really appreciate everything he did to help me with this journey! I just want to thank him for everything!"

Mia Wilson – my grade soon went from a C+ to an A.

"I have been in Spanish class since eighth grade, and it has been my hardest class year after year. Memorizing the conjugations and vocabulary felt like an impossible task. I would read my textbook over and over. I would repeat words to myself to try and learn the definition. I would even watch YouTube videos to try and learn the grammar rules. Nothing would stick in my brain, and my Spanish grade was dropping by the second. I was losing motivation and seriously considering giving up trying to learn.

I felt overwhelmed by the material in my classes (especially Spanish). Every time we started a new unit, I was still unconfident about the last unit and felt like I was behind the rest of my class. I hated going to Spanish class because I would be so scared that the teacher would call on me, and I wouldn't know what she was saying. I was losing all motivation to continue trying to learn. Whenever I had a big test coming up, I would often cry because of how overwhelmed and stressed I was since I didn't know any of the material.

After taking this course, I used the memorization techniques on my next Spanish vocabulary quiz and aced it. My grade soon went from a C+ to an A. I felt much more confident in my study skills and the system I was studying. I am now excited to go to my Spanish class, and I feel like a star student. I am extremely impressed with myself and the results of this course.

Thanks to Stephanie and Cosimo for giving me the confidence and skills to be a better learner and student. I am very grateful for this course, and I would not be where I am today if I had not taken it."

I could include more than 1000 testimonials annually from around the world, but I want yours to be the next one. I can't wait to hear your story. Most important is not your past but where and who you want to be now!

Acknowledgments and Tips

If you have ever written a book, it takes so much **time, effort, ideas,** and **love.** If you're thinking of writing a book, here are a few tips on never giving up.

Effort because you have to be able to summarize years of expertise, experiences, and what your life-changing mentors did for you.

Ideas since everything starts with an idea. I really thought this can be revolutionary for any student, parent, professional, or individual who wants to take their life to the next level. I have the pleasure of serving my ideas to the world.

Time. There are times when the words come and when they don't. Just connect with yourself, go for a walk for ten minutes and enjoy the sun, then come back, and you're ready. I think the most important resource we have is time. As my dear friend and mentor, Luca, told me, "Everyone has time, but the way we use it makes all the difference. You can spend ten minutes being happy and the rest frustrated, or one minute of frustration and the rest on your mission. Decide hour by hour, then minute by minute, then second by second how you want to feel. This can create happiness by choosing minute by minute how you want to feel. You're your heaven and hell; nobody else is responsible for this, only you and you alone."

Love. I feel nothing but love every time I think about what lightbulb moment you have had reading some of these chapters.

I love how much this changed my life and how much this will impact yours.

Love drove my fingers down on every letter of my keyboard.

Yes, if you meet me on YouTube or Instagram or wherever, there are people who call me crazy, but I believe you have to be crazy enough to build a dream.

I want to thank Luca Lorenzoni, who is always my ally, friend, and mentor. The person who made this possible for me, who allowed me to find the courage, and in Latin, courage means use your heart. I put my heart beyond my fears. Thank you, Luca, for always being there for us.

I want to thank my wonderful wife and instructor, Stephanie. When I tell her you're the perfect one for me, it is real. You don't know her and if you meet her, you'll love her, of course not as much as I love her, but you'll love her. I want to thank her since if it wasn't for her patience, strength, faith in us, and passion for our dream, I wouldn't be here; she was the one who, when I was learning 6,000 words in two weeks, was laughing at my pronunciation of words like "beach" and was reminding me that everything would be perfect.

I want to thank Giacomo Navone, who inspired me to write this book without hesitation and contributed so substantially. I want to thank him from the moment I became an instructor, and he believed in me, destroying the crippling self-doubt that I was too young, inexperienced, and dyslexic to do it. Thank you, Giacomo, for always being there for our family and me.

I want to thank Simone Sacco, the witness at my wedding and great friend who pushed me to open this American location.

I want to thank my team of mentors and managers, including Carol Johnson, Rori Grosse, Maddy White, and Melina Sardar. They always grow and improve the way to change people's lives and have believed in this adventure since the beginning when it was nothing more than an idea.

I want to thank all the people who, despite my heavy accent at the beginning of my journey, loved us and allowed us to impact more people's lives:

- ✓ Bob Snyder, founder, and CEO of Renatus, visionary and inspirator
- ✓ J Stark, President of Renatus, who always believed in possibility and solutions
- ✓ Renatus's entire team of outstanding professionals
- ✓ Jan Fishler for her patience and time in shaping this book.

I want to thank Michael Huggins for putting love before fear. My best friend, a brilliant and wise counselor who pushed my dream one step further.

I want to thank Dr. Michelle Mras for helping me transform my accent with her superpower and believing in what I could not see yet.

All the volunteers for my study cases chapter who will inspire you to new possibilities: Tom Robinson, Michael Huggins, Damon M. Greene, Gabriela Picazo-Batista, and Mia Wilson.

I want to thank all our customers and collaborators who believed in our dream month by month and are always there to support.

And lastly, I want to thank my mom, Michela Manisi, my dad, Ciro Intermite, my brother, Gabriele, all of whom supported me and my dream from across the Atlantic. Your love knows no distance.

I hope you enjoyed this book, and I can't wait to see you and learn about your story with your astounding results.

I strongly recommend you reach out to me on Instagram, TikTok, Facebook Messenger, YouTube, my website or email. I want to share in your success, be connected to your energy and be part of this family of people changing the world.

Cosimo

Dedication

(Rori) Aurora Grosse
Ace Lee
Alex Kures
Alex Oleynikova
Alex Winningham
Alfred Ramirez
Amanda Romine - Nelson
Amy Carr
Andi Pellicci
Andre Simoneau
Andrew Castine
Angie Perkins
Becca Tomlin
Billy Gulliermo Samour
Bob Gazaway
Bob Snyder
Brenda B Bailey
Carol Alegre
Carol Johnson
Chelsie Haue
Cheryl Lee
Chris Deal
Chris Tyrrell
Christian George
Christopher Keith
Cindy Coleman
Connie Presson
Dalton Barton
Dan McKenzie
Daniel Austin
Danielle Butler
David Lee
Dawn Nokomis
Demetrios Tzortis
Dhru Beeharial
Dipankar Disgupta
Donna Grace
Douglas Hermann
Dr Michelle Mras
Earl Co
Eileen Lee
Elizabeth Alabassyan
Eric Counts
Felipe Pulino Côrrea
Gabriel Soares
Gabriela Picazo-Batista

Gary Barnes
Gayle Friend
Gillian Edward
Greg Kimble
Heidi Christianson
J. Stark
J.L. Flack
Jacob Householder
Jan Fishler
Jane Kramer
Jane Reynolds
Jay Jacobs
Jean T. Tucker
Jenna Manchego
Jeremy Farrell
Joe Nazario
Joe Rinderknecht
Judy Hahn
Judy O'Higgins
Kambi Jecminek
Karen Millerwise
Kaz Aylott
Keely Austin
Kelly Jones
Ken Rochon
Kevin Menne
Kim Allen
Kimberly Gibson
Kittie Gazaway
Kyle Carney
Laura Campbell
Laura Hackle
Leslie Householder
Lindsey Cowen
Lisa Bennett
Lisa Jenkins
Lisa Potter
Lorraine Conaway
Maddy White
Mara Dowler
Marilyn Lamer
Mary Gaul
Masha Oleynikova
Maurine Kures
Melina Sardar
Melissa Ivey

Mia Wilson
Michael Huggins
Michael Steinberg
Michelle Torres
Miles Stephens
Misha Schryer
Nancy Delain
Natasha Garrett
Nate Dickson
Nate Jecminek
Nick Young
Nicole Berzins
Nikita Oleynikova
Patrice Madrigal
Peggy Smith
Rayana Starre
Rebekah Thomas
Rina Gelzinis
Rita Boccuzzi
Ryan Ngyuen
Sarah Tzortis
Sebastian Roesch
Sharon Lewis
Sheila Fitzer
Shelley Sims
Stephanie Hastings
Stephanie Sperring
Stephen Replin
Steve Hunter
Steven Kirch
Sumary Ohelman Centeno
Suzy Lewis
Sydney Jackson- Clockston
Tienne McKenzie
Tina Kulp
Tina Teach-Myer
Tom Robinson
Tomika Davis
Trevan Householder
Trisha Beharie
Umear Haq
Veronica Perez
Yas Haq
Zach Gaeta
Zach Ohelman
Zack Shamy

Afterword by Michelle Mras, PhD

Imagine what you would accomplish if you could tap into the full potential of your brain function. Your search is over. The mental shifts you have read within the pages of this book are life changing. Long held beliefs you have about your mental capabilities should have been challenged, and now can be conquered.

This idea seems farfetched, I know. Even after you have performed the exercises presented in this book, you will experience disbelief. I thought the same thing when Cosimo Intermite explained the Genius in 21 Days course to me. As a traumatic brain injury survivor, I have learned a lot about the processes and capabilities of a brain. For over two years, I was unable to speak or walk without assistance. I went through several therapies in order to retrain my brain to complete everyday functions. When I learned about the Genius in 21 Days program, I was hesitantly optimistic. How could someone like me benefit from brain training with a brain that was not fully functional?

Once I finally accepted the invitation from Cosimo to attend the Genius in 21 Days program, it was a game changer! There were techniques and brain games that I was surprised to discover worked repeatedly. Once my mind accepted that it was doing what I was convinced it couldn't do, I was freed from my inner-critic voice that claimed I had a damaged brain. My brain worked far better than I thought and was performing tasks I never dreamed it could do.

I'm excited that you are holding this book. I asked you earlier to imagine what you would accomplish if you could tap into the full potential of your brain function. Now, imagine how your life would be like if you never developed the self-doubt about yourself. Be ready to embrace the fundamental change in how you view your ability to learn.

Remember that change is an emotional journey. It's not rainbows and butterflies in a field of daisies. Change is uncomfortable and forces you to evaluate who you are. The beauty is in the possibilities.

Prepare to unleash the best version of you… Unapologetically.

AMPLIFLUENCE
AMPLIFY YOUR INFLUENCE

You're the Expert, but are you struggling to Monetize your Authority?

Amplify Your Influence in 3 Sessions

Speak
Your Message

Publish
Your Message

Convert
Your Message

Authors and Speakers often find themselves struggling to build a strategy that actually makes them money.

Check Out
All Of Our 'Live'
Tour Stops

amplifluence.com

SCAN FOR
TOUR INFO

More Books From

www.PerfectPublishing.com

More Books From PERFECT PUBLISHING

www.PerfectPublishing.com

Made in the USA
Monee, IL
08 March 2024